Psychotherapy: A Very Short Introduction

VERY SHORT INTRODUCTIONS are for anyone wanting a stimulating and accessible way into a new subject. They are written by experts, and have been translated into more than 40 different languages.

The series began in 1995, and now covers a wide variety of topics in every discipline. The VSI library now contains over 350 volumes—a Very Short Introduction to everything from Psychology and Philosophy of Science to American History and Relativity—and continues to grow in every subject area.

Very Short Introductions available now:

Available soon:

For more information visit our website

www.oup.com/vsi/

Tom Burns and Eva Burns-Lundgren

PSYCHOTHERAPY

A Very Short Introduction

OXFORD
UNIVERSITY PRESS

Great Clarendon Street, Oxford, OX2 6DP,
United Kingdom

Oxford University Press is a department of the University of Oxford.
It furthers the University's objective of excellence in research, scholarship,
and education by publishing worldwide. Oxford is a registered trade mark of
Oxford University Press in the UK and in certain other countries

© Tom Burns and Eva Burns-Lundgren 2015

The moral rights of the authors have been asserted

First edition published in 2015

Published in the United States of America by Oxford University Press
198 Madison Avenue, New York, NY 10016, United States of America

British Library Cataloguing in Publication Data
Data available

Library of Congress Control Number: 2014947151

ISBN 978-0-19-968936-1

Printed and bound by
CPI Group (UK) Ltd, Croydon, CR0 4YY

Contents

Preface

Psychotherapy, psychology, and psychiatry

What is the difference between psychotherapy, psychology, and psychiatry? Most people find them hard to distinguish, which isn't surprising. The terms seem to be used interchangeably about the same activities, and some people describe themselves as practising more than one. Many psychologists and psychiatrists are also psychotherapists, and there are even the odd individuals who are all three. There are already *Very Short Introductions* (VSIs) on psychology and psychiatry, so we should start by distinguishing these subjects and explaining what this VSI to psychotherapy will add.

Psychology is the science of mental processes and behaviour. It uses all the standard scientific methods of observation, experimentation, and theory development. It isn't even restricted to humans—many psychologists study animal behaviour, both for its own sake and also to model human thinking. Psychologists examine emotions, perceptions, thoughts, etc., and increasingly use very high-tech equipment such as computers and brain scanners. Some 'clinical' psychologists work in health services and apply what they learn from their science to help people with problems.

Psychiatry is a medical discipline. Psychiatrists first train as doctors with the full range of exposure—general practice, surgery, obstetrics, etc. When qualified they then specialize in psychiatry, which is defined as the diagnosis and treatment of mental illness. While modern medicine is very 'scientific', it is not first and foremost a science. It uses several sciences such as physiology, genetics, and biochemistry to advance its knowledge and practice, but its fundamental approach is observational, not theory driven. Psychiatrists do not start from experiments or theories but from the problems people bring to them, which they then attempt to categorize and find treatments for. Psychiatry is firmly wedded to the ideas of diagnosis and treatment, although mental illness, and in particular the boundary between health and illness, are often very controversial.

Psychotherapy is a form of treatment for emotional and psychological problems that is based on talking and understanding. It relies on two (sometimes more) individuals exploring the problems the patient or client brings. The aim is to gain greater understanding of the problems and better ways of dealing with them. Many psychotherapists use psychiatric diagnoses and the term 'patient', but they think more in terms of personal problems and identity. They do not prescribe medication. Like medicine, psychotherapy is not primarily a science, but more a skills-based profession, which uses various theoretical concepts to understand human experience and development. Like medicine, it also consists of many different approaches and techniques, and this book will describe and discuss those that are most significant.

The growth of psychotherapy

Roy Porter, a historian of medicine, called the 20th century 'the century of psychiatry'. He could just as well have called it 'the century of psychotherapy'. In the period of these hundred years both have transformed from obscure, minor activities to topics of enormous public interest and investment. Psychiatry now accounts for about one-fifth of all medical costs throughout the world. Psychotherapy before World War I was an exotic practice restricted to rich intellectuals and their psychoanalysts. The war changed all that. Psychological treatments for emotional disorders altered psychiatric practice fundamentally and began to change society's thinking. By the mid-20th century, psychotherapy had become a constant feature in artistic and cultural debate, but more importantly it had become recognized as an effective treatment for a wide range of emotional and interpersonal problems.

Psychotherapy is now widely available—not just within psychiatry and not just for mental illness. Psychotherapists are to be found in hospitals, schools, universities, prisons, and increasingly in some enlightened workplaces. People seek their help for longstanding problems, but also for crises and relationship difficulties.

Psychotherapy or psychotherapies?

Psychotherapy has never stood still. It has not only expanded its range and extent, but there have been exciting and lasting changes in its practice. The traditional psychoanalytic psychotherapy described at length in Chapter 2 dominated the earlier years, but various styles and adaptations evolved up until World War II. The Nazis' persecution of the Jews (almost all the early psychoanalysts were German-speaking Jews such as Sigmund Freud) drove psychotherapists abroad to the US, South America, and the UK. The result was a variation in practice in different societies and the beginning of radically different ways of thinking (see Chapter 3). Since the war we have witnessed the establishment of time-limited therapies (Chapter 4), the exponential growth of counselling, psychotherapy's less formal relative (Chapter 5), and more recently the rapid development of a strikingly different approach called cognitive behaviour therapy (CBT, Chapter 6). As psychotherapeutic thinking became bolder it began to escape its traditional one-to-one format and experimented with group and interactive therapies (Chapter 7).

Just how different are these therapies from each other, and how much are they variations on the same theme? Is counselling just another form of psychotherapy, or is it something quite new and different? In writing a book like this we have described the differences, so that you can get a sense of the range. Many practitioners insist that they are radically different from each other, but we are not convinced. Our view is that they have more factors in common than separate them. All have the same starting point in their commitment to help fellow human beings who are struggling with distressing problems. All assume that things can get better, and that an honest, reliable, and tolerant relationship can provide a setting for change. Lastly, all are based on some form of belief that what matters in our lives is not simply what happens to us, but crucially what we make of it and how we deal with it, often based on mental processes we may only be dimly aware of. Psychotherapy aims to bring these processes into clear consciousness—to help us make sense of them and take more control of our lives.

Gender and terminology

It struck us in writing this book just how skewed the sexual representation was. More women seek psychotherapy than do men, and many more psychotherapists are women than are men. Yet when we were writing about who developed this or that psychotherapy, or who wrote what, it has tended to be dominated by men. We believe this is a historical legacy of the discrimination that characterized professional and educational opportunities in previous generations. We predict that any book covering the same ground in fifty years time will be peppered with creative women writers and scientists.

Gender stereotypes have played a significant (and not especially honourable) role in psychiatry's history, so this is not unimportant. In the text we wanted to avoid the clumsy his/her but were not happy with just using 'he, him, his' throughout. Redressing the balance by always using 'she, her, hers' seemed equally artificial. We have opted to simply vary the gender in a random way. There is no hidden pattern in it, so don't try and work it out!

You can please some of the people some of the time ...

Psychotherapy is an intellectually vibrant activity. It never stands still and is full of debate and disagreement. Psychotherapists are committed people who have undertaken long and demanding trainings, and who almost invariably are very passionate about their work. Any book that sails a middle course in describing them risks offending everyone. We have ensured that each of these chapters has been read by at least a couple of real experts in their areas. Invariably they have thought that we did not accord their therapy type quite enough space or importance. That is the nature of the beast. We both have our own specific therapy trainings (Eva in cognitive analytic therapy, and Tom in group analysis), so we know how they felt. However, our job has been to try and give you a balanced overview and we hope that we have. We have chosen to describe some therapies in more detail where we feel they illustrate underlying principles particularly well, not necessarily because they are the most important approaches.

A final word of warning. This is not a self-help book. There are plenty of those around and many are excellent. This VSI may help you decide which of the various types of psychotherapy appeals to you if you are thinking of seeking help. But that is all it can do. Psychotherapy, and particularly counselling, is now much more accessible and the old stigma that used to be attached to seeking such help is, mercifully, shrinking fast. So if you are thinking of talking things over there is absolutely nothing to be lost by making the move, and it could make all the difference. A good place to start is usually to discuss matters with your family doctor, or to access the websites of reputable psychotherapy organizations. Currently, psychotherapy registration is not statutory in most parts of the world, but responsible therapists would welcome you enquiring into their level of training or accreditation. We would recommend meeting with two or three therapists for assessment sessions before making a final decision on whom to see. Psychotherapy is a very personal business, and the 'fit' between you and your therapist will play a crucial role both for the experience and for the outcome of the process.

List of illustrations

Chapter 1
What is psychotherapy and who is it for?

The rise of psychotherapy was one of the most striking features of the 20th century. What started as an obscure treatment for wealthy, intellectual neurotics in *fin-de-siècle* Vienna has changed not only the nature of psychiatric practice but how we understand ourselves. Psychotherapeutic language and thinking is now part of everyday life, and we hardly get through a day without using it: he 'made a Freudian slip', their relationship 'is a bit Oedipal', my 'inferiority complex' is showing. Counselling is now seen as a natural response to many of the problems in our lives.

Our parents' image of a psychotherapist—if they had any at all—was probably that of a bearded psychoanalyst with his patient lying on a couch (see Figure 1). Psychotherapy is now much less exotic, encompassing marriage guidance, cognitive behaviour therapy (CBT), Alcoholics Anonymous (AA) meetings, group therapy, and much more. It is a very broad church, which has existed in the practice of traditional healers from long before Freud, indeed before psychiatry itself.

What links the sober psychoanalyst, the careful and scientific psychologist, and the mystical and dramatic shaman? At its most basic psychotherapy involves using an agreed relationship with specific characteristics, involving a trained practitioner and a

1. The image of the traditional bearded analyst with the mittel-European accent sitting behind the couch dominated our view of psychotherapy for many decades

patient, to obtain relief from emotional suffering. Most Western psychotherapies are based on talking and discussion. They aim for a very personal understanding of the origins and meaning of problems in order to remove symptoms and obtain relief. Not all emphasize understanding the causes; in fact, existential philosophies do quite the opposite. Some discourage such a search for unique personal meanings, and some psychotherapies rely on a dramatic discharge of emotion.

The core feature of any psychotherapy, however, is the *relationship* between a practitioner and a patient, a relationship which inspires hope for healing or change. Both need to share an understanding of the process and agree to work together within that relationship. Confidentiality is the norm, as therapy often involves exploring very personal thoughts and feelings which people may feel conflicted about or ashamed of. Psychotherapists are expected to be worldly-wise and tolerant. They will be familiar with the extremes of human experience, hard to shock, and slow to blame.

How long or how intensive psychotherapeutic treatment is can vary enormously—from a handful of meetings to the (now very rare) classical psychoanalysis of an hour a day, five days a week, for several years. Therapist training can also range from several years to shorter part-time courses. Psychoanalytic schools require an intensive, and expensive, personal analysis. Psychotherapies are sometimes called 'talking cures' or 'psychological treatments'. These terms are used to distance current practice from psychoanalysis and its unscientific reputation, but they are too broad for our purpose. They lose the focus on the relationship and self-understanding of psychotherapy. For example, teaching someone about their illness and how to manage it (psycho-education) is technically a talking treatment, but it is not psychotherapy as we would understand it. We will retain the term psychotherapy to indicate the skilful and deliberate use of a specialized relationship to gain self-understanding and relief from troubling symptoms.

Who is it for?

In Freud's day, patients usually sought help for very severe, often dramatic, symptoms. His patients had to have a high level of education and drive to be taken on for psychoanalysis. Treatment was very intensive and rather intellectual. It delved into internal conflicts, making links between symptoms, unconscious wishes, and disturbing early experiences. By making these conscious (becoming aware of them) the patient could gain greater control. Current psychoanalytic practice focuses more on problems in relationships and self-fulfilment, and is sought by a much wider range of people. This is not surprising. Our happiness depends most of all on our relationships, so if they go wrong, we want to understand why and try to repair them.

Not only are those who seek psychotherapy now more varied, but it is provided in a much wider range of settings, including in family doctor practices and occupational health schemes. It is no longer restricted to 'intellectuals', and accepts patients with more pervasive difficulties, such as self-harm and substance abuse, as well as those from more disturbed or deprived backgrounds.

Much has been made of *psychological mindedness* (the ability to reflect and think about thoughts and feelings) as a requirement for psychotherapy. We think this is putting the cart before the horse. People often seek therapy precisely *because* they are not able to reflect on their lives in a psychological manner. Psychotherapy can provide the tools to develop this capacity. The popularity of the more transparent and 'democratic' recent therapies such as interpersonal therapy (IPT), solution focused therapy (SFT), and cognitive analytic therapy (CAT) (Chapter 4), and CBT (Chapter 6), testify to this trend, as does the increasing use of written aids and questionnaires.

Psychotherapy in the 21st century is more accessible and varied than it was a hundred years ago, and this book will reflect that scope—from the unique and specialized to the more generic and familiar. We will restrict ourselves to the forms of psychotherapy generally available for adults. Child psychotherapy is a very specialized activity with its own theories and practices, and neither of us is an expert in this field. While early psychoanalysis did not see older adults as suitable candidates for analysis, this view has changed, and many current psychotherapy models are suitable for this age group and for people with learning disabilities. Although there is a growing body of psychotherapy practice for these groups, we will not address them in this book.

Before we provide an outline of present-day psychotherapy, we think it might be helpful to trace its lineage and put it in its historical context.

Psychotherapy before the discovery of the unconscious

Modern psychiatry began just over 200 years ago at the end of the 18th century. It is a product of the Enlightenment, when reason and logic triumphed over religious dogma. People began to trust their own experiences to understand the world around them. Two iconic events marked psychiatry's beginning, one in France and one in England.

In Paris, in 1789 after the French Revolution, Philippe Pinel took charge of two enormous institutions and 'struck off the chains from the insane'. He was convinced that their brutal treatment made their disturbances worse, rather than reduced them. In England at about the same time a Quaker family, the Tukes, were appalled at practices in their local madhouse. They established an alternative, the York Retreat, providing a calm and tolerant setting where patients were kept busy and constantly encouraged. Punishment and harsh treatments were expressly prohibited. They called this approach *moral treatment*.

The success of the York Retreat became world renowned. Along with Pinel's fledgling attempts at the classification of mental illnesses, it formed the basis of modern psychiatry and the asylum movement that was to dominate it for the next century and a half.

At this time a remarkable individual, Anton Mesmer (1734–1815), was revolutionizing how we treat those who, although not 'insane', suffered from severe emotional problems. He used light hypnotism, which was originally called *mesmerism* after him. His treatment relied on powerful suggestion, using his force of personality.

During sessions his patients often became overwhelmed by strong and inexplicable emotions, after which their symptoms might disappear. This looked very similar to the exorcisms used by the church, but Mesmer's rejection of religious explanations was the turning point. His treatments initiated the rational investigation of psychological processes that we now take for granted.

Mesmerism rapidly evolved into deep hypnotism, where patients discovered hidden emotional conflicts during trance states. Along with post-hypnotic suggestion (following instructions of which one appears to be totally unaware), this obliged a rethink of the understanding of the mind in order to accommodate unconscious processes. Until then the mind was the sum of what you were conscious of thinking or feeling at any moment. René Descartes' 'cogito ergo sum'—I think therefore I am—conveys this view. Yet powerful forces and complex ideas were clearly in operation beyond the reach of our day-to-day awareness. Hypnosis had also demonstrated that such unconscious thoughts were involved in neuroses and could be used in their cure.

Exploring the unconscious and the birth of psychoanalysis

Hypnosis and suggestion became central to the treatment of neuroses in the early 19th century. While Mesmer relied on drama and showmanship, others were more reflective, recognizing the importance of trust and suggestibility in the process. By the 1850s hypnosis had fallen from grace, tainted by its association with spiritualism and fraud. It came back into favour with the work of Jean-Martin Charcot (1825–1893), a celebrated neurologist in Paris. Hysterical disorders were common at that time. They included paralyses, blindness, anaesthesias, strange movements, and even epileptic fits with no obvious physical cause. Charcot acquired an international reputation in treating hysterical seizures using hypnosis (see Figure 2). Freud, like so many aspiring neurologists, visited him and was very impressed.

2. *Une leçon clinique à la Salpêtrière*, Andre Brouillet, 1887.
Jean-Martin Charcot (1825–1893), the famous Parisian Neurologist,
using hypnosis to demonstrate hysteria. Freud visited him and copied
his methods

Back in Vienna, Freud began to use hypnosis and suggestion to
treat his neurotic patients. Despite some initial success he soon
realized that powerful suggestion followed by emotional release
did not always work. For many patients the detailed nature of
their unconscious conflicts had to be understood. Initially he
believed that neuroses were caused by childhood sexual abuse,
which gave rise to memories that had to be kept unconscious
because they were too distressing. Later he changed his opinion
and came to believe that the abuse was imaginary, and that the
neurotic symptoms really arose from unacceptable impulses and
drives. Psychoanalysts created relationships with their patients, in
which it was safe to dive deep into the unconscious and confront
what previously had been too threatening. Unconscious processes
had become firmly established as the source of neuroses, and the
substance of psychotherapy.

In the first half of the 20th century, psychotherapy essentially
meant psychoanalysis. There were various adaptations—shorter

7

forms, group, and even institutional forms—but the basic principles were the same. Their aim was to guide the patient on a journey through their unconscious and to make links or 'interpretations' between experiences in earlier relationships and current problems. Other than during the two world wars, when it was conscripted to deal with shell shock and battle casualties, psychotherapy remained the preserve of the intellectual and the wealthy.

After World War II, society changed rapidly and new psychotherapies were developed to reflect this. Psychoanalysis had itself contributed to these changes, with its emphasis on the universality of emotional conflicts and complexes, and its demonstration of the benefits of emotional honesty. It now stressed the importance of early childcare and explored real relationships, not just painful memories. With an increasingly egalitarian society it became inevitable that such benefits should be made more widely available. Psychoanalytic psychotherapy responded with shorter and less intensive treatment regimes, once a week for a number of months rather than daily for several years. However, the changes soon to come were even more fundamental.

Psychotherapy in the present day

The problems we bring to psychotherapists (depression, anxiety, difficulties with relationships, and self-doubt) may not have changed that much. However, our expectations are now very different. The stiff upper lip has given way in a society that prizes emotional expression and self-revelation. People expect to be happy and they aspire to be so. The American Constitution promises 'Life, Liberty, and the Pursuit of Happiness', and most of us expect just that. This is very different to the world of duty and acceptance that had shaped Freud and his patients. He explicitly rejected happiness as a goal for therapy. For him, and his generation, the measure of good mental health was to be able 'to love and to work' (*zu lieben und zu arbeiten*). Indeed, he stated that the aim of psychoanalysis was 'to transform neurotic misery into common unhappiness'! This clearly will not do for our modern tastes.

Personal fulfilment, self-expression, happiness, and control over our own fate are the reasons most of us now seek out psychotherapists. It is not just our aspirations that have changed. Modern society is more mobile and fragmented, with dispersed families often unable to provide support, and traditional religion playing a reduced role in giving comfort. Individuals now need help with coming to terms with themselves as much as they do with difficult relationships. Psychotherapy has changed and diversified to meet these needs.

Counselling

In times of distress we need to be listened to and feel understood, and counselling provides a kindly and tolerant ear. Counselling has become available to those who would never have considered themselves as 'neurotic' or candidates for formal treatment with psychotherapy. It provides help for ordinary people facing problems in everyday life or in their relationships. Counselling was established by the work of Carl Rogers (Chapter 5). He called it *client-centred* or *person-centred* to emphasize its independence from rigid theories and dogma. It provides a calm, safe, and supportive relationship that allows self-reflection and emotional healing. Rogers recognized that simply having time to ponder your feelings and thoughts is enormously valuable in its own right.

The relationship between counselling and psychotherapy is complex and shifting and there is no simple, universally accepted description of their differences. People argue about whether it is a form of psychotherapy or a quite different activity altogether. It is generally less ambitious than psychotherapy, with its goals less fixed and the process more directed by the patient. In client-centred counselling the therapist resists imposing structure. Counselling speaks to a universal human need, as is shown both by the number who seek it out and the number who seek to practise it. People like counselling, and they like being counsellors. Many do it without payment in organizations such as the Samaritans and Relate. Training is variable but generally quite short.

Counselling is also an integral part of many wider treatment regimes. Drug and alcohol counsellors draw heavily on their personal experiences of addiction to guide clients and sustain hope. Traditional client-centred practice ('how does that make you feel?') often alternates with forceful challenges in such rehab programmes. In hospitals and self-help groups for patients with physical illnesses, counselling helps in managing the illness, coping with anger and distress, and reducing isolation and hopelessness. Counselling after personal trauma (such as assault or rape) and major disasters (such as train crashes or earthquakes) is also regularly offered.

CBT and focused therapies

There are some radically new psychotherapies. The most widespread and influential of these is CBT, which is outlined in detail in Chapter 6. CBT focuses directly on current thoughts and actions (hence 'cognitive' and 'behavioural') more than on feelings and personal history. It identifies unhelpful thinking patterns and challenges them utilizing specific techniques, often practised between sessions. The aim of therapy is more control and mastery than in-depth understanding. Treatments are usually weekly for twelve to twenty sessions, sometimes even fewer. The relationship is very equal and transparent, stressing collaboration, and is devoid of mystique.

CBT's 'technological' quality is probably its most significant break with the past. Out goes the long training analysis and the mysterious and aloof manner. In comes the therapy manual and democratic engagement, with repeated exercises and measurement. CBT is probably now the most widely practised therapy in healthcare and has a strong evidence base for treating anxiety and depression. Its therapists see no conflict between 'drugs' or 'therapy', and are quite comfortable with 'drugs and therapy'.

Sorting different therapies neatly into tidy boxes risks caricaturing them and oversimplifying. In truth there has been a steady process of development, refinement, and diversification of all therapies. Several have made radical changes in theory and practice, although clearly with links to psychoanalysis. Examples of this group (taken up in Chapter 4) are IPT, DIT, and CAT.

Group and family therapies

Much of psychotherapy is directed at understanding the problems people have in relation to those around them. In individual psychotherapy the therapist has to rely on what the patient tells her, and this can be pretty one-sided. Several therapies have broken through this barrier, and involve relevant other people directly in the treatment. This can be by working with naturally occurring groups, such as in couples or family therapy, or by bringing together groups of individuals with similar problems, as in group therapy. We are social animals and we come alive in our relationships, so these psychotherapies can be dramatic and fast moving.

Family therapy was first used in the treatment of disturbed children and adolescents. Sometimes a child's disturbance is a symptom of a wider family dysfunction which needs to change. Even where this may not be the case the whole family may be affected and need help, as when a child is gravely ill. Treatments can sometimes be very short, involving only a handful of meetings. Family therapy usually focuses on current relationships rather than digging into ancient history, and the emphasis is on the structure of the relationships. The same is true of couples and marital therapy. What is locking family members into sterile and repetitive conflicts? How can they escape to something more supportive and liberating?

Harnessing the power of the group has become a central plank in addictions treatment, such as in AA. Self-help organizations form the mainstay of support in alcohol and drug abuse worldwide, and they have spread to other addictions such as gambling.

Most therapy groups are composed of individuals with similar problems, but not all. The original group therapies brought together a range of individuals seeking self-understanding and change. Some groups are psychoanalytic in orientation, but most are more direct and exploratory. The group benefits from the variety of individuals and problems it contains, as members learn about themselves and experiment with new ways of relating and being.

Interactive therapies

All the newer psychotherapies are more active than psychoanalysis. Freud wanted to understand his patients' mental processes and was keen to avoid contaminating them with his presence. This gave rise to the 'blank screen' therapist, who strove to reveal nothing about himself by word or deed. Later psychotherapists are less concerned about this and believe a well-timed active intervention can move things along. More interactive therapists are particularly needed with less 'typical' psychotherapy patients. The 'right' sort of psychotherapy patient was flippantly described as YAVIS—young, attractive, verbal, intelligent, and successful. Clearly not all who need psychotherapy fit this narrow caricature. Children, less introspective individuals, those with less education, and those with less self-confidence or motivation may need more active help.

Some therapies are based entirely on action, such as music therapy, dance therapy, art therapy, and drama therapy (Chapter 7). These activities may be healing in themselves. Intensely self-conscious children and adolescents can lose themselves in music or dance, freed temporarily from doubt and anxiety. Alternatively, the therapist may use the activity as a platform for exploration: 'Tell me about your painting. Why such dark colours?' 'Hamlet's speech seemed to stir you up—what do you think he was getting at?'

There is a wide range of therapeutic activities and exercises that overlap with psychotherapies. These include meditation, encounter groups, massage therapies, and more. Many are very sophisticated, and it can be very difficult to make a clear distinction between them and 'psychotherapies proper'. How can we decide what is and is not a psychotherapy, and which to include in this book? We have relied heavily on 'psychotherapies proper' being individually tailored to each patient and their specific problems. Activities or exercises which are equally useful for anyone (such as yoga or meditation), while undoubtedly very good for us, are not included here.

New ideas and psychotherapy's horizons

Completely new psychotherapies have arisen to meet modern man's sense of alienation. Existential psychotherapies, which are outlined in Chapter 5, reject preconceptions about how we ought to be. They aim to liberate us from what they see as a futile search for meaning. Having accepted the randomness, even absurdity, of the universe we must find fulfilment in our own unique existence. This ultra-modern emphasis on 'being through becoming' is derived from philosophers such as Kierkegaard, Buber, and Sartre, but is surprisingly close to therapies that draw on ancient Eastern philosophies.

Eastern thinking emphasizes the constancy of change and universal connectedness. Personal fulfilment and enlightenment come from self-awareness in the moment with the abandonment of desire. Several Western psychotherapies have incorporated such ideas. Jung wrote of the wholeness of existence and attaining integration by abandoning striving. Gestalt therapies work towards a sense of wholeness rather than concentrating on detailed concerns. One of the most rapidly spreading forms of cognitive therapy, mindfulness-based cognitive therapy (MBCT), draws heavily on Buddhism. Patients meditate and concentrate on the moment, practising tranquil self-awareness.

Current psychotherapies draw inspiration widely, well beyond psychoanalysis and standard psychological theories. Your choice of therapy may be based as much on your temperament and philosophy as your symptoms. The no-nonsense thrusting businessman may choose CBT or transactional analysis, while the more artistic individual might seek a Jungian analyst.

Risks in psychotherapy

When you read articles comparing psychotherapy with antidepressants, they always list the side effects and risks for the pills. Psychotherapy is assumed to be risk free: 'It may not always work, but it can't do any harm'. This is not so. Any effective treatment carries risks. Longer psychotherapies carry a risk of overdependence or inertia. Issues can also be opened up which feel overwhelming and result in increased distress, perhaps with a retreat into alcohol or even self-harm. Good psychotherapists know this and carefully assess patients' character strengths and supports as well as their problems before embarking on treatment.

Freud advised against psychoanalysis with psychotic illnesses or very severe depression, and most psychiatrists and psychotherapists would still agree. Exploratory psychotherapy is always unsettling to some degree, so balancing the potential benefits against the stress involved should never be neglected. If recovering from a severe mental illness, or alcohol or drug abuse, it may be best to wait.

Most countries are trying to develop formal registration for psychotherapists, to restrict membership to those with an adequate training and with clear procedures for excluding incompetent practitioners. However, it is an imperfect system and does not yet cover all psychotherapists. In addition, psychotherapy is not an official profession, so anyone can in theory call themselves a psychotherapist.

The privacy and confidentiality of psychotherapy can lead to a loss of perspective. Relatively minor problems can become magnified or, conversely, emerging issues can be missed because of the familiarity that comes with the relationship. The therapist's personality can have profound effects, particularly if he or she is not fully aware of it. For this reason most psychotherapists regularly meet with another colleague for supervision, even long after they have finished their formal training.

There is also the rare risk of improper sexual conduct by therapists. The intimate and private nature of all medical practice brings such risks. This can be even more pronounced in psychotherapy where intimate wishes and longings are ventilated, and where dependent and anxious patients can come to idealize their therapists. Practitioners have always taken these risks seriously, hence the existence of rigorous professional codes with severe sanctions.

The best defence is to rely only on well-trained psychotherapists who are members of established professional associations. This guarantees not only their basic competence but also that they are in regular contact with colleagues. Isolation is the danger— psychotherapists go astray much more often when they work alone, especially in private practice. However, we should not exaggerate these risks. Most therapists have their networks and supervisors, so such incidents, while still indefensible, are very rare. Finding a good therapist is not that difficult if you take soundings and get advice. The following chapters will describe in more detail the thinking and practice of the most common psychotherapies and what kinds of problems they can help with.

Chapter 2
Freud and psychoanalysis

Almost all modern psychotherapies owe their origins to Freud and psychoanalysis, although listening to psychotherapists talk you could be forgiven for not believing it. Psychotherapists are a fractious bunch, given to arguing over fine points of theory and splitting into ever-smaller schools of thought. This ought not to surprise us. Psychotherapy is a very personal activity. You have to be fully engaged in it to do it well, so it is difficult to be dispassionate.

Throughout this book we describe how various therapies differ from one another, so that you can get a grasp of them. In truth they have much more in common. What can seem to be very diverse practices, using strikingly different languages, often draw on a common set of processes and lead to similar outcomes.

Psychoanalysis is no longer the commonest, nor indeed the dominant, psychotherapy, but it has a unique place in its history and development. Psychoanalytic principles and practices have influenced virtually all subsequent therapies. Getting a grasp of them will help you to understand what follows, so we will describe them in considerable detail. Let us begin with the remarkable man who started it all.

Sigmund Freud (1856–1939)

Sigmund Freud was born in Freiberg, in what is now the Czech Republic, to a Jewish wool merchant and his much younger third wife who doted on her son. From the age of nine he lived in Vienna, at that time the liberal and cosmopolitan capital of the Austro-Hungarian Empire. The studious and talented Freud excelled at his schooling and became a doctor and subsequently a neurologist, carving out a promising career as a researcher.

He met his future wife, Martha Bernays, in 1882 and promptly became engaged. He needed to earn a decent salary to get married so he took a clinical post in the Vienna General Hospital. He managed to continue researching part time, and published on the properties of cocaine and on some neurological disorders. All neurologists, then as now, are regularly confronted with the puzzle of whether a patient's symptoms result from nerve damage or from underlying psychological problems. Neuroses, especially *hysterical disorders* as they were called then, produced a range of apparently inexplicable and disabling physical symptoms such as paralyses, weaknesses, pains, and fits.

Married in 1886, Freud established a private practice specializing in neurotic patients, many with these hysterical disorders. He lived and worked in the same spacious apartment for forty-seven years until he was driven out by the Nazis in 1938. By that time he was a very sick man and died in London a year later. A very domestic individual, Freud was sober and predictable in his habits, invariably dressed in a tweed suit. His only obvious vice was smoking cigars, which eventually caused his fatal cancer of the mouth. He was inordinately proud of his six children, particularly his youngest daughter Anna, who became a noted child analyst.

In 1885–6 Freud spent four months visiting the world renowned Jean-Martin Charcot in Paris. Charcot specialized in distinguishing hysterical from epileptic fits and used hypnosis to induce and control the seizures. Freud was very impressed, and on his return to Vienna began to use hypnosis in his practice.

Psychoanalysis begins to take form

Freud's use of hypnosis continued for some years. He would put his patient into a light trance and, placing his hands on their temples, suggest that their symptoms were becoming weaker or that power was slowly returning to a paralysed limb. However, in 1896, along with Joseph Breuer, he published five detailed case histories, *Studies in Hysteria*. In these they used hypnosis not so much to cure the disorder but to gain an understanding of it, to reveal the underlying neurotic conflicts.

Freud's attention had moved from removing symptoms to trying to understand the causes behind them. This preoccupation was never to leave him, and it has remained central to most psychotherapy practice. Freud was not the first to recognize the role of the unconscious in neuroses, but he stands out because of his total commitment to identifying the *causes* of the symptoms. He was committed to honesty and insisted on sharing the unvarnished truth with his patients. Psychoanalysis aimed to explore unconscious mental processes. What were its tools?

Free association and dream interpretation

Abandoning hypnosis, Freud began to encourage his patients to relax and say whatever came into their minds. To help them relax they lay on a couch, and he sat just out of view (see Figure 3). Uncomfortable or disturbing thoughts and feelings—which had been actively suppressed in the unconscious mind—could then bubble up, evading the usual controls. He called this process *free association*. A similar process occurs during sleep when repressed thoughts make their way into consciousness, albeit exotically disguised in dreams.

3. Freud's consulting room around 1910. Patients would have no chance of being unaware of Freud's personality and interests when lying in this room

Freud called what we remember on waking the dream's *manifest* content. The dream's real meaning, its unconscious *latent* content, has been distorted in its journey to consciousness by several recognizable processes. These include *condensation* when a single image serves to convey a number of different concerns, or *symbolization* when a vivid image stands for an unacceptable preoccupation. One rather hackneyed example is dreams of trains being understood to symbolize sexual intercourse. Analysis was needed to uncover the latent content.

Searching out the clues to neurosis revealed in dreams and free associations remained the basis of all Freud's subsequent work. He believed that nothing was ever truly forgotten, and that nothing was ever just coincidence, hence the 'Freudian slip'. Everything had a meaning, and that meaning could be uncovered by analysis. Over his lifetime Freud radically changed many of his ideas about mental mechanisms, the origins of neurotic symptoms, as well as practical aspects of psychoanalysis. However, he never deviated from his search to *understand* and uncover unconscious conflicts.

19

The most distinctive feature of psychoanalysis is the *interpretation*. An interpretation is when the analyst helps make the link between unconscious meaning and motivation, conscious experience, and behaviour. Clarifying these links promotes insight into the previously obscure origins of current difficulties. The patient can then respond more rationally to issues in her life.

Infantile sexuality

Freud initially believed that the hysterical disorders in his women patients were the result of sexual abuse in childhood, often by their fathers. Over time he came to doubt this explanation. He concluded that these stories of abuse arose from fantasies, from the child's desire for an intense, intimate relationship with her father. To explain this he proposed that right from birth we have strong instinctual (sexual) drives, which he called the *libido*.

Freud proposed that the libido developed through several stages culminating in the *Oedipus complex*. Around the age of three to five years the child struggles to have an exclusive and intense relationship with the parent of the opposite sex and experiences the other parent as a rival. This rivalry and jealousy generates the Oedipal triangle.

Freud believed that it was possible to become stuck at any of several earlier developmental stages, and that this would prevent healthy maturation. He saw the successful resolution of the Oedipal triangle as essential for mature sexuality. This was necessary for forming realistic and affectionate adult relationships, and to tolerate sharing. Those who did not resolve it were trapped into seeking unrealistic, exclusive, and oversexualized relationships.

Mental structures: the ego, id, and super-ego

Freud became interested in the mental structures that shaped and modified these strong instinctual drives. He believed they arose in the primitive and chaotic unconscious mind—what he called the *id* ('it' in Latin). They both influenced and were controlled by the more rational conscious mind, the *ego* ('I' in Latin). Freud proposed a third structure, the *super-ego*, for our self-critical and controlling behaviour—our conscience.

He initially thought the super-ego was derived from our parents. However, the scathing self-criticism he observed in severely depressed patients made him question its rationality. His solution was to conclude that while it was derived from the ego (representations of our parents and upbringing), it was powered by the id, which contributed its primitive intensity. Many analysts (such as Melanie Klein) now believe that this intensity is because the Oedipal conflict actually takes place much earlier. Consequently, the super-ego acquires some of the characteristics of the fearsome monster of a small child's nightmares, rather than just an overly strict parent.

Freud's final addition to mental structures was the concept of *defence mechanisms*. These are our mental mechanisms to deal with unwelcome unconscious thoughts and feelings on a day-by-day basis. Unlike the repression in neurosis, these do not require constant energy to hold the threatening thoughts and feelings out of consciousness. Defence mechanisms become stable parts of the personality—reliable, automatic ways of dealing with uncomfortable issues as they arise. Defences include *denial* (as in the alcoholic who bluntly insists he has no problem), *projection* (where an angry person claims he is 'just fine' but everyone around them is furious), and *splitting* (which deals with complex relationships by making one person the good guy and the other the villain).

Exploring defence mechanisms became an important part of psychoanalysis. Initially they were seen simply as a resistance to analysis, which had to be overcome to get to the underlying conflicts. They later came to be seen as key features of a patient's character whose understanding was helpful in its own right.

A particular aspect of treatment that troubled Freud was when patients idealized him, especially when they declared they had fallen in love with him. He called this *transference*, believing it was the transfer of emotions from previous important relationships on to the current therapeutic one. He initially saw it simply as resistance, but over time came to believe it is an essential part of treatment—a vital route into the unconscious.

Transference analysis is now a central feature of all psychoanalysis. It uses the patient's responses to the therapist as a guide to how they experience their other relationships and themselves. It also includes analysing *counter-transference*, the feelings evoked in the therapist by the patient. Interpretations which link the transference relationship with the patient's life situation and simultaneously with important past experiences are considered to be the most potent. Counter-transference work enables psychoanalysts (and psychoanalytic therapists) to work with adults who are less verbal, or even young children seen with their parents.

The spread of psychoanalysis

All the early analysts in Vienna were Jewish (Carl Jung in Switzerland was the first non-Jewish practitioner). The rise of Nazism in the 1930s forced them to leave for the US, the UK, and South America, where they established many psychoanalytic institutes. Theories developed and disagreements lead to splits. The most acrimonious was the early departure of Carl Jung, whose thinking (see Chapter 3) had always incorporated spiritual dimensions. This grated with Freud's more reductionist emphasis on the role of sexuality. Numerous other 'schools' of psychoanalysis have developed, many long-since faded away.

In the US the 'neo-Freudians' and 'ego-psychologists' established a strong presence, with figures such as Karen Horney, Erich Fromm, Alfred Adler, and Harry Stack Sullivan. They proposed a broader understanding of the origins of neuroses, emphasizing the role of culture and social influences. In the UK Melanie Klein's approach effectively bypassed the ego to interpret primitive emotions and fantasies right from the start. She was also one of the first to use psychoanalysis with children.

More recently, the French psychoanalyst and philosopher Jacques Lacan has profoundly influenced psychoanalysis in much of continental Europe and Latin America. A prodigious intellectual, Lacan's writings are incredibly difficult to understand and some of his practice eccentric. For instance, his analytical 'hour' always started late and lasted only as long as he thought it useful or productive.

Psychoanalytic training

Psychoanalysis is very strict about who can call themselves analysts and about what training and supervision is required. In the 1920s Carl Jung insisted that analysts should have their own training analysis. Nowadays the training is demanding, involving several years of training analysis, attendance at seminars, and close supervision of early treatments. This protracted and expensive training is thought by some to make analysis too rigid and inhibit originality. It certainly makes analysis expensive.

Being in analysis: once a week or every day?

Few analysts see all their patients five days a week. It is neither affordable nor compatible with modern lives. Most patients have one or two sessions a week. Some analysts consider this an unavoidable compromise, and that difficult patients still need a 'full analysis'. The majority have adapted to less frequent sessions and consider the advantages to probably outweigh the disadvantages. The experience may not be so intense, but it focuses the minds of both partners and allows time to reflect and reality-test between sessions.

Some time ago we both shared a flat in south London with a trainee analyst. He headed off before seven in the morning to Hampstead, five mornings a week, for his analysis. He then came back to his full-time job as a psychiatrist, before returning to Hampstead to his patients or seminars every evening, to come home exhausted at nine or ten at night. We often joked with him that he could not have anything to speak about in his sessions other than the analysis itself and the traffic jams between us and Hampstead! His experience was that this very intensity allowed him to delve deeper into personal understanding without daily life intruding too much. This 'time out' from normal life, inhabiting a different mental zone, is undoubtedly a special quality of a full analysis. But what should one expect from weekly analytic treatment, often called *psychoanalytic* or *psychodynamic* psychotherapy?

The first sessions

The first session will be devoted to finding out why you have come. The therapist will introduce herself and explain that she is there to listen to you. She will work with you to help you understand your problems better, so that you can find solutions to them. She will usually outline how the process works and give you some idea of what to expect. Sessions are likely to last an *analytic hour* (50 minutes) and to be at a regular time each week. The 50-minute hour gives the therapist time between patients to write notes and ensures that each session starts on time.

Analytic therapies use punctuality and regularity to provide a sense of structure and security around what can be an emotionally harrowing process. Regularly coming late or missing sessions will be seen as evidence of *resistance*—that you are trying to avoid painful issues. Analytic psychotherapists are strict with all routines and boundaries and rarely permit contact between sessions. Even if you are very upset at the end of a session you will be encouraged to contain your emotions until the next one. Living with, and trying to understand, powerful feelings is part of the treatment.

Most therapists will offer a small number of exploratory sessions before you both decide whether or not to continue. Your therapist is likely to be relatively silent, but that does not mean that she is not listening. Everything said in the room is confidential. Confronting painful issues can temporarily increase distress rather than reducing it, and it is important to stay engaged. That the analyst does not rush to comfort you does not mean at all that she is indifferent, but rather that she wants you to have time to better understand what is going on. All that is expected of you is to try and be as honest as possible.

Having outlined the process the therapist will encourage you to talk about your problems. 'Tell me in your own words what is going on in your life and why you are here. Just describe it, don't try to explain it, and take your time.' Many people find this first session highly emotional, often bringing an enormous sense of release, with words and emotions flooding out. The therapist will not interrupt much in the first session. This is not a time for detailed clarification but for getting an overview; your emotions are as much a part of this as your story.

Therapists usually take care to wind up the first session in good time. This allows them to summarize and discuss with you any thoughts they have about what you have said, for example:

> The relationship you describe with your partner seems to be burdened with anger, possibly carried over from your disappointment with your father. You have shown me how upsetting it remains for you, and that probably needs to be better understood. We will need to continue with this next time.

This reviewing also allows time for you to move back out of the emotionally intense world of psychotherapy and prepare to face the everyday world as you step outside. Do not be surprised though, if you do not get any clever summary or psychological 'diagnosis'. Many therapies have identified assessment sessions, but analytic therapy has a much more open-ended approach to how long treatment will last and what will be worked on.

Free association, interpretation, and working through

In psychoanalytic therapy you will remain very much in the driving seat. The therapist will not tell you what you should or should not talk about. *Free association* (saying whatever comes into your mind) is still the cornerstone of the treatment. This is matched by the analyst's *free-floating attention* to themes that emerge in what you choose to talk about. You are nowadays more likely to sit in a chair and face your therapist than lie on a couch. You will also be encouraged to report and discuss your dreams.

Analysts believe nothing you say is random. It is all important and it stems from the preoccupations that are troubling you, but which you may be trying to avoid. The meaning will become clear in time, as long as you are patient and do not rush it. This sounds self-indulgent and easy but it is not. Most of us can find the apparent lack of structure very stressful initially, and want the therapist to be more directive. Very often in the beginning we experience our mind as being totally blank. The analyst may reply that it is almost impossible 'not to think', we should just take time, and the thoughts will surface.

Analytic psychotherapy is based on the premise that if we understand what is going on in our minds, then we have the possibility to change it—in Freud's words, 'where id was, ego shall be'. So analysis aims above all else for self-understanding, for *insight*. Over time the therapist will increasingly make interpretations to promote insights. Imagine describing the surprising anger you felt when your partner forgot your birthday:

It was ridiculous. I know he has been very busy, and I know he loves me, but when he sat there chattering away and clearly had completely forgotten I felt hate, real hate. I wanted to scream at him or pack my bags and leave. Yet he is considerate and affectionate and I knew perfectly well he had been preoccupied with the house repairs. How could I feel such hate over something so trivial?

The therapist might link this to your earlier descriptions of a sense of neglect when you were growing up:

This sounds very similar to how you described feeling left out and ignored by your father when your sister was ill. How hurtful it felt, yet because of the worry about your sister you could not have a tantrum or tell your dad. Could there be a link with that pain and not just the forgotten birthday?

Interpretations help us recognize how our responses (whether thoughts, feelings, or actions) are so damaging or distressing. This is because they relate not just to what is happening now but also to earlier, unresolved, and formative experiences. They are rarely blinding flashes of insight that instantly clear away the fog of neurosis. They have to be repeated, building up a richer understanding of what are well-entrenched, complex patterns of thought and behaviour. The most effective interpretations are believed to be those that illuminate the similarities between important past relationships and current experiences in both your day-to-day life and in what is going on in the analysis itself—the transference. Such triangular interpretations (see Figure 4) are sometimes called *mutative* interpretations because of their power to stimulate change.

Using such links there is the possibility of *working through* the pain of past experiences—coming to terms with them and moving on. Working through is the main task of therapy; more time-consuming and less glamorous than the interpretations, but

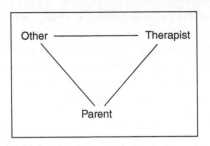

4. Triangle of persons

essential for personal growth and healing. In working through, the transference relationship to the analyst assumes a central role. Old feelings of anger, despair, rejection, or resentment that have festered under the surface for decades are reignited and experienced in the room. The analyst is the object of these feelings and must withstand them, neither retaliating or wilting under their attack, nor rushing to remove discomfort.

The concerned but relatively reserved manner that analysts adopt, the *blank screen*, makes it possible to project transferred emotions on to them. However, they should be blank but not absent—without trust and a sense of security in the relationship such projection would be altogether too frightening to engage in. The relationship must have enough depth for these storms to be both weathered and confronted while new patterns are evolved. Working through enables us to make the hugely important shift from understanding the problem intellectually ('I see that this has upset me because I tend to believe that nobody is capable of helping me') to really feeling it ('I really did feel unloved and unsupported—yet now I sense that people in my life *can* help me').

Analysis of defences

Latterly, analytic therapists have focused more on helping us understand our habitual defence mechanisms—the patterns we regularly use to deal with things that would otherwise make us

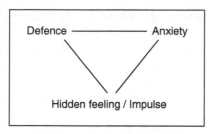

5. Triangle of conflict

uncomfortable. So rather than going straight for the troubling conflicts underlying our neurotic problems, they may examine our routine ways of dealing with these uncomfortable issues. The two are not mutually exclusive and most therapists will do both. Sometimes work on defence mechanisms is needed in order to get to the underlying conflicts. A patient may, for instance, routinely intellectualize their problems, denying the emotional impact of them:

> I realize that he has been too busy to remember my birthday; he's been altogether far too busy. I just got a bit irritated because I worry he is not looking after himself enough and allowing time for himself.

Several sessions may be needed to understand the origins of this intellectual defence and the underlying conflict or feelings (see Figure 5).

When is enough? The ending of therapy

Traditional psychoanalysis can go on for years. There is no fixed limit—you carry on until the work is finished. Woody Allen once quipped after seeing his analyst for fifteen years, 'I'll give it one more year and then I'll go to Lourdes'. Most analytic therapy nowadays is time-limited, although not a rigidly fixed number of sessions.

The analyst David Malan, who inspired the triangles used in Figures 4 and 5, pioneered a sharply focused thirty-session analysis, sometimes referred to as 'short-term psychodynamic psychotherapy'. However, it is more likely that at the start you and the therapist will agree to see each other for a defined period, say once a week for twelve months, and then review.

Having an end in sight right from the beginning focuses the mind and avoids coasting along with no sense of urgency. Too much urgency, however, would inhibit the free-floating exploration essential to psychoanalytic work, so a balance has to be struck. A year seems a long time at the start, although it may not feel like that as the time approaches. The ending of therapy is often experienced as its most productive period.

Ending can be painful, even if the therapy has done its work— perhaps especially if it has. Strong feelings about the therapist are common, often of an idealizing nature, as they have been experienced as understanding and tolerant. The goal in analysis is to end with a balanced view of the therapist—neither all-knowing and wise, nor cold and insensitive. Achieving such a neutral appraisal while continuing to separate is difficult, so a 'wobble' is common towards the end. The gains may seem to be lost and symptoms may suddenly recur. This is a sign that the work of ending is underway, not a reason to delay it or to prolong therapy.

Who benefits most from psychoanalytic psychotherapy?

Those who go into analysis or psychoanalytic psychotherapy, particularly in private practice, are a highly self-selected group. This is a form of therapy that appeals broadly to those who are interested in the life of the mind or their internal world for its own sake. They may want increased self-understanding almost as much as they want relief from symptoms. It would be wrong to believe that you have to be some sort of intellectual to benefit, but the therapy is challenging and does require intellectual curiosity. It is best suited to those with difficulties in relationships in general rather than one relationship in particular, or with a gnawing dissatisfaction with their lives rather than isolated anxiety attacks. Psychoanalytic psychotherapy is certainly no quick fix. It is not for the impatient, but it can undoubtedly turn lives around when it works.

Chapter 3
Post-Freudians: moving towards the interpersonal

The early development of psychoanalysis was a period of intense intellectual ferment. Freud's ideas were evolving rapidly and he collected a glittering group of followers. Initially they were all men; creative, self-confident, and argumentative. They rapidly began to generate their own ideas, often falling out with each other, and several split from Freud. The first to leave the group was Alfred Adler, but the most acrimonious and influential split was with Carl Jung.

Carl Gustav Jung

Jung was the first non-Jewish psychoanalyst and the first one not from Vienna. He lived in Switzerland working as a psychiatrist with Manfred Bleuler, the psychiatrist who introduced the term schizophrenia. Jung was twenty years younger than Freud, tall and wealthy, and their relationship was very intense until it soured.

Jung had always been somewhat mystical. Unlike Freud he came from a religious family, and his earliest interest had been in paranormal phenomena. He eventually fell out with Freud over what he saw as Freud's excessive emphasis on the role of the sex drive, but also more generally as a reaction to Freud's unremittingly rational approach. Jung was fundamentally a romantic individual who believed that analysis had the potential to bring patients to an emotionally richer, more spiritual state.

Jung's constant striving for something more, and his dissatisfaction with the mundane, characterized both his thinking and his life. He broke sexual boundaries with patients and during a particularly turbulent period he probably tipped over into a brief psychosis. Despite all this (or perhaps because of it) he was enormously productive and creative. He introduced the concepts of introvert and extrovert, but he is probably best known for his ideas on symbolism.

Jung took a radically different approach to the unconscious material that patients reported in their analyses. He was one of the few early psychoanalysts who worked in a psychiatric hospital, and had noticed similarities with the hallucinations described by psychotic patients. He observed regularly recurring images of easily identified figures, such as that of a wise old man, a warm motherly figure, God, and the Devil. Freud thought of these as distortions caused by neurotic conflicts, but Jung believed they were fundamental to human thinking. He called them *archetypes*, and believed that they could be found in all cultures and all times. He concluded that we access them from a *collective unconscious*, a folk memory that we are all born with and which shapes us.

Prominent archetypes include the *anima* (the feminine side of men), the *persona* (the face we present to the world), and the *imago* (our ideal self). The *shadow* is particularly important in Jungian thinking. It contains all our most shameful and frightening experiences, thoughts, and feelings—those that we keep hidden both from ourselves and from others. Jung thought that our shadow grew stronger and more threatening the longer it was ignored (like Oscar Wilde's ageing portrait of Dorian Gray). For us to develop healthily it needed to be brought into the daylight and confronted.

Jungian psychotherapy is called analytical psychology to distinguish it from psychoanalysis. It is shorter, usually with weekly sessions for a year or so, and there is no analytical couch. Therapist and patient sit facing each other and therapy is much more focused on the here-and-now. Analytical psychology aims for integration of the personality, aspiring to a harmony which accepts inherent contradictions rather than striving to reduce or eradicate them. As in classical analysis, the initial sessions involve an exploration of early experiences, and dreams are also taken very seriously. However, this early exploration is soon brought to bear in understanding current experiences and problems. In sharp contrast to psychoanalysis, dreams are taken at face value with no tortuous extraction of latent from manifest content.

While Freud was fairly modest in his aims for therapy ('to convert your neurotic anxiety into day-to-day misery'), Jung believed it could make us better people. His emphasis on personal integration, his preoccupation with symbols and Eastern mysticism (see Figure 6), and his tolerance of uncertainty, have meant that Jungian psychotherapy is particularly attractive to creative and artistic individuals and also to people later in life.

Freud thought that we become less able to utilize psychotherapy with increasing age, because we become more rigid. Jung, on the contrary, believed that the wealth of life experience older people bring makes them eminently suitable for psychotherapy. Jungian psychotherapy provides opportunities to make sense of life and come to terms with ourselves and our approaching mortality. Because of its tolerance of ambiguity and mystery, it is often experienced as richer and more tolerant than analysis.

Alfred Adler and the neo-Freudians

Alfred Adler was one of Freud's original inner circle. Although also a Viennese Jew he was very different from Freud. He came from a large Hungarian family (Vienna was still the capital of

6. The mandala—an Eastern spiritual symbol of the universe and wholeness. Jung wrote in his memoirs: 'I sketched every morning in a notebook a small circular drawing... and discovered what the mandala really is:... the Self, the wholeness of the personality, which if all goes well is harmonious'

the Austro-Hungarian Empire) and was short and physically unimposing. His politics were radical and his personal habits chaotic. His lasting contribution to psychotherapy is the *inferiority complex*. He also thought that Freud overemphasized the sexual, and believed that what drove most of us was a struggle to overcome a sense of personal inferiority, whether real or imagined.

Adler was very energetic and forthright. He actively spread his ideas throughout workers' education movements, schools, and various other institutions. He situated the patient firmly as a whole person in his social context, and believed that you had to understand this context in order to understand the individual. He often interviewed family members and encouraged frank exchanges between them. Many of his ideas about social inclusion and the power imbalances in society (especially that between the sexes) seem strikingly modern. He saw neurotic symptoms as barriers to achievement and self-fulfilment, and would often start his therapies with the question 'If you didn't have this problem, what would you be doing?'

Neo-Freudians

Adler moved to the US in 1930 and was followed by many Jewish psychoanalysts fleeing the Nazis. These arriving analysts were exposed to a dramatically different lifestyle in America and were taken aback by it. The impact of culture and the wider society on them and on their patients was revelatory. The effects of society and culture in shaping patients' aspirations, their values, and also their neuroses could not be ignored. Neo-Freudian practice and writing embraced a broader, more interpersonal, perspective.

This attention to social factors in psychotherapy was not a trivial departure. Karen Horney, an early member of the group, challenged the entrenched gender stereotypes of psychoanalysis, as have many feminists since. She attacked its prejudices against women and the demeaning concept of 'penis envy'. She even argued that male ambition and competitiveness were themselves a form of envy, an envy of women's innate creativity in giving birth. The shift in thinking was profound.

Psychotherapy was becoming firmly located as an *interpersonal* activity. Its focus was moving to the current interactions between the patient and the individuals who mattered to them. Painful memories from the family past were no longer the whole story. Just as a patient's relationships determined their well-being, so their interaction with the therapist became key to successful psychotherapy. These interactions were seen as agents of change in themselves, not simply tools to understand intrapsychic events. Another in this group, Harry Stack Sullivan, declared that psychotherapy should 'focus on the interactional, not the intrapsychic'. Therapists should pay attention to the real events in their patients' lives (which he called 'problems in living'), not just to patients' interpretations of them. For later existential therapists such as Irving Yalom (Chapter 5) the relationship itself came to be seen as curative.

Erik Erikson

The neo-Freudians had initiated a process that would, in time, lead to counselling and person-centred therapy. Erik Erikson helped set this transformation on its way by radically rethinking the maturational crises we experience in our lives. He proposed that we continue to face new challenges to our sense of identity throughout our lives, calling them the eight stages of development. Problems can arise at any of these stages, even if earlier ones have been resolved perfectly well. For example, Erikson believed that we can develop serious psychological disturbances when confronted by a crisis such as a serious illness, despite having been perfectly well adjusted previously. This is in stark contrast to traditional analytical thinking where such late-onset psychological crises are explained as reactivations of unresolved earlier conflicts.

Erikson, despite his name, was also a German-speaking Jewish analyst from Vienna. He was tall, blond, blue-eyed, and had been taunted from an early age from both sides (Aryans about his

Box 1 Erikson's stages of psychosocial (ego) development

Completed	Failed	Age
Trust	Mistrust	0–1 years
Autonomy	Shame	1–3 years
Purpose-initiative	Guilt	3–6 years
Competence-industry	Inferiority	6–11 years
Fidelity–identity	Role confusion	12–18 years
Intimacy	Isolation	18–35 years
Generativity	Stagnation	35–64 years
Ego integrity	Despair	65 years onwards

Jewishness, Jews about his Aryan looks). His work reflects this experience. His eight stages in life each present us with a potential *identity crisis* (Box 1). Each of these identity crises contains two opposites that have to be recognized and accepted, with both making their unique contribution to who we are.

Obviously these ages are just rough indications. Erikson's stages provide a structure for understanding problems that takes age and experience into consideration, and even later challenges and stages have been added more recently to his original eight in response to working with our increasingly ageing population. Erikson did believe, like Freud, that getting stuck in personal development later in life was more likely if earlier conflicts had not been resolved. However, he also believed we could break down later in life, even if all the earlier conflicts had been surmounted. For instance, a successful and well-balanced man who has been enormously productive in his career might still struggle with the end of that career. His 'generativity' may become eroded by the 'stagnation' in his leadership position.

Daniel Stern, an American analyst and researcher, came to an intermediate position, based on close observations of mothers and babies. He described different *domains* in the development of our sense of self. He viewed each of these domains as tasks for life that are never fully resolved, and so we revisit them repeatedly. Like Erikson, he also stressed the importance of attending to the 'present moment', in therapy as in all our relationships.

Shell shock in World War I

There is a clear intellectual thread running from Jung to the neo-Freudians. Practice steadily shifts away from a tight focus on what is going on in the patient's mind and its origins in very early experiences. The interest settles more on what is happening right now, both between the patient and the therapist, and also more widely in the patient's life. These were, however, not the first variations in Freudian practice. During World War I, psychotherapy came into its own during the treatment of shell-shocked soldiers (Figure 7), although the military psychiatrists using it did not have much time left over for writing up their theories.

World War I produced an enormous number of psychological casualties. This was mainly because of its special nature—months of waiting around in trenches, always on edge for the next sniper bullet or shell to land. Most soldiers had only a limited education and were psychologically unsophisticated. Many developed what we now easily recognize as hysterical disorders—uncontrollable shaking, paralyses, and nightmares that made them unfit to fight. These conditions became severe and chronic because they were unable to make the link between the onset of their symptoms and the very understandable terror they were experiencing.

A slimmed down and modified Freudian approach was rapidly developed for treating shell shock. This abandoned Freud's sexual

7. The great numbers of soldiers who developed shell shock in the
trenches demonstrated that psychological stress could cause
breakdowns and psychological treatments were needed to help them

theorizing and focused on emotional conflict. Symptoms originated from the soldier's sense of duty and his 'unacceptable' (and thus repressed) desire to escape the horror of his current situation. Like the later neo-Freudians, the army doctors worked towards rapidly uncovering these repressed desires and fears. However, they were not interested in, nor did they have time for, fine details. They relied heavily on their status and force of personality to reassure and encourage their patients, often using simple hypnosis to strengthen suggestions. An important feature of this rough and ready psychotherapy was normalizing the experience for the soldiers and protecting their self-respect.

This down-to-earth and more supportive analytic relationship features widely in novels, but has received relatively little attention in psychotherapy literature. It demonstrated a pragmatic and self-confident approach by doctors familiar with Freud's and Jung's psychodynamic thinking.

Attachment theory

A similar leap forward occurred after World War II, with the creation of *attachment theory*, proposed by John Bowlby. Bowlby was an analyst familiar with the work of leading animal behaviourists. He had been sent away early to boarding school by his rather cold, upper-class family, and was acutely sensitive to the importance of separation for young children. He undertook groundbreaking investigations into the lives of displaced children in the aftermath of the war.

In his highly influential book *Maternal Care and Mental Health*, Bowlby stressed the importance of a consistent and warm early bond with the mother for emotional development. His insights have revolutionized the care of children in day nurseries and hospitals across the world. He emphasized the importance of the quality of this real relationship rather than the infant's fantasies about it—such as the real experience of abandonment, deliberate or otherwise—and this initially made him unpopular with analysts.

His concept of *secure* and *insecure attachments*, which provide us with internal working models for subsequent relationships, is now widely accepted. The sense of security experienced in therapy is now seen as a *reparative* experience, one that has some potential to make up for an earlier inadequate attachment. It sees the secure attachment to the therapist as a healing factor in its own right. Cure does not come exclusively from intellectual insights enabling the working through of earlier conflicts. These conflicts may simply lose some of their power as a direct consequence of this new healing experience.

Donald Winnicott was a prominent psychoanalyst and paediatrician who also linked actual events and experiences in real relationships with our personal development. He introduced two influential new ideas. The first was that of the *good-enough mother*. She should not be too perfect or there would be no scope for spontaneity and change. Equally, she should not be too chaotic or there would not be sufficient security and containment for emotional growth. Being 'good enough' means accepting those natural flaws and minor failures, which we all need to learn to tolerate and master. His second idea was the *false self* that a child might develop in response to a mother or carer whose own needs are too strong and intrusive. If this happens then a false self, which is often overly mature and seemingly self-confident, is presented to the world like a shield. A consequence is that the *true self* becomes isolated from experience and is deprived of opportunities to develop fully.

These developments may seem a bit academic, but they have had an enormous influence on psychotherapy and more widely on how we manage our personal and family relationships. What is characteristic of all of them is the elevation of the importance of real experiences in the process of psychotherapy. The reality of the mothering experience matters as much as, if not more than, any fantasies and conflicts surrounding it. What sort of life the patient is living now also matters—whether or not she has the potential to establish and maintain close and fulfilling relationships.

Lastly, the tone of the psychotherapy matters, not just its success in the technicalities of uncovering conflicts or interpreting defences. The psychoanalyst Nina Coltart stressed how 'people not only like, but need, to tell their stories, especially to an attentive listener equipped with certain skills', someone who 'listens in a particular way'. Freud believed that the analyst should be a neutral figure, and that any transference was to be understood and interpreted away. Now it is no longer considered a failure of therapy if the patient comes away with a fond memory of the process and a genuine affection for their analyst.

Psychotherapy has moved permanently away from the caricature of an exciting, intellectual detective story, tracking down and unearthing the hidden cause of problems. The relationship itself matters. The therapy relationship is usually experienced as warm and positive, but it is most emphatically not *just* that. The therapist's job is to use it to work with relationship patterns and behaviours, many of which may be quite painful. Analysts still insist that the treatment should not be too comfortable—patients have to confront difficult issues. However, virtually all psychotherapists now recognize that the quality of the relationship matters in its own right and is a major part of the cure. In all of the therapies described in the following chapters you will see this understanding run through their practice.

Chapter 4
Time-limited psychotherapy

Early psychoanalytic treatments were often brief. Freud treated two of his most famous patients over a very short period: 'Dora' only for eleven weeks and the 'Rat Man' for eleven months. He saw the composers Bruno Walter and Gustav Mahler for only six and four session each. Some of his contemporaries attempted to develop shorter treatments as well as varying the analytic technique to make it more active.

Despite this, psychoanalysis demonstrated a remorseless lengthening. Further innovations, such as the development of the transference neurosis and regression, required extensive working through. The passive analytic stance increased the risk of dependence in longer therapies. Psychoanalytic training added a further pressure by requiring extensive personal analysis and lengthy training cases. Brief therapies are also more demanding to conduct, and their greater turnover of patients adds to professional uncertainty. Brief therapy came to be seen as second best or inferior.

In recent decades interest has grown in the development of shorter or time-limited psychotherapies. Originally initiated by psychoanalysts, this development has been accelerated by accumulating evidence for the effectiveness of time-limited therapies, especially CBT. It had regularly been observed how change occurs most often either in the early stages of therapy or when the end is in sight, but that focus can be lost in the middle stages. This also contributed to the drive for shorter therapies.

Cost-effectiveness pressures and the need to provide evidence-based treatments identified, for example, by NICE (National Institute for Clinical Excellence) in its guidelines for the UK's health services, have coincided with demands from patients for shorter treatments. For many of us, therapists and patients alike, short-term therapies are now the treatments of choice, rather than a necessary compromise. The IAPT programme (Improving Access to Psychological Therapies) in the UK, which offers short-term, mainly CBT-based therapies, has consolidated this development. A number of time-limited psychotherapies have emerged with increasing evidence for their effectiveness but also with plenty of 'sibling rivalry'. Let us start by outlining what they have in common.

Common features of brief psychotherapies

'Psychotherapy should be as short as possible and only as long as the patient really needs it' writes Angela Molnos. The aim of therapy is 'to create a special place in which the past can appear in the here-and-now, a space in which past emotional conflicts are re-lived and understood with clarity, and in which new solutions to old problems are found'. Common factors include weekly, face-to-face sessions with a more active therapist, and with a clear focus on problem patterns as they present. Depending on whether the therapy is more psychodynamic or cognitive in nature, the use of transference will vary, as will the emphasis on problem solving. Dynamic approaches are more likely to pay attention to attachment and loss during the ending of the therapy. Therapies also vary in how much they follow a detailed manual outlining practice. CBT practitioners often value them, whereas brief psychodynamic therapists rarely rely on them.

The shortening in brief therapies is most noticeable in the early sessions. Patterns of thinking and feeling are identified and are challenged very early on. Problematic personal and interpersonal patterns do not require much digging to find—if we only look carefully, they are there in all our interactions. The therapist may notice how the person enters the room (striding in or shuffling, looking the therapist in the eye or avoiding her gaze, talking non-stop or having to be drawn out) and feed this back. Such habits reflect the person's lived experience, and how this shows in the present provides food for thought. Observations like these lie at the core of the therapeutic process, and are returned to regularly.

To illustrate these points and give a flavour of brief or time-limited therapies, we describe three common, but distinct forms. IPT was devised specifically for depression. CAT is an integrative approach, combining cognitive understandings and techniques within a more analytic framework. SFT is an active approach, which engages people's inbuilt ability to find solutions. As Chapter 6 is devoted to CBT, it will not be included here.

We find that making a distinction between brief therapies and time-limited ones is helpful. Brief therapies usually last for one year or less but there is quite a degree of flexibility. In time-limited therapies the number of sessions or the length of therapy is explicitly determined at the outset. Most time-limited therapies are also brief but they do not necessarily have to be.

Interpersonal psychotherapy (IPT)

IPT was developed in the US in the 1980s by Myrna Weissman and John Markowitz, specifically for people with depressive illness. It has been shown to be very effective with patients who are either not helped by medication, or are unwilling to take it. The term 'illness' is used quite deliberately here. A central feature of IPT is explaining that the patient is suffering from a medical illness, thereby giving her temporary relief in the 'sick role'. This reduces self-blame and guilt, and helps patients to accept that they are not at fault for feeling the way they do. It also confirms that this is a well- recognized and treatable condition, and thus helps to instil hope. IPT also includes psycho-education about the illness and its various treatments as part of the protocol.

Despite its very medical language IPT insists that mood and life situation—and especially relationships—are closely interrelated. Patients are helped to make links between life events and the onset of their depression. IPT has an explicit relationship focus, and the patient's aims for therapy are usually linked to bringing about changes in their relationships. Therapy is based on common therapeutic factors such as developing a strong treatment alliance and emotional engagement, so that patients can feel understood and supported during a difficult phase in their lives. However, the therapy relationship is not explored in any detail as in psychodynamic therapy.

IPT links the emergence of depression to commonly occurring and disturbing life events. These are grouped as *losses* (or *bereavement*) such as the death of someone close, *role transitions* such as significant changes or life upheavals, or *role disputes* which are conflicts or struggles with important people. IPT goals are to reduce or remove depressive symptoms, to improve interpersonal functioning, and to resolve interpersonal problems. The therapist pays particular attention to how patients communicate their needs and feelings to others. They also help patients to repair their social supports, which are often lost in the withdrawal from contact so common in depression.

IPT is limited to between twelve and sixteen sessions, and is highly structured with a defined beginning, middle, and end. The therapist and patient start by conducting an *interpersonal inventory*. This lists in detail the important relationships in the patient's life, such as with partners, parents, or children.

They examine the emotional quality of these relationships with close attention to the feelings both within and between the people involved. They will explore patterns of interaction and communication, especially if conflicts are experienced. Does the other person, such as a partner, help the patient manage better or actually make the problem worse? The therapist will use all indications, in both verbal and non-verbal communication, to establish possible links between the relationships and the onset of symptoms. Together therapist and patient try to understand the 'why now?' while also identifying any underlying personal vulnerabilities or predispositions. The goal of the beginning phase is to create a joint formulation of the problem—what may have caused it as well as what keeps it going. A common pattern is a vicious cycle of depression leading to lowered self-esteem, resulting in social withdrawal, in turn leading to loneliness and increased depression. We all recognize what it is like to feel miserable, embarrassed, or ashamed and so not to want to trouble others. The result is that we don't make that call to a friend or ask for help.

The work of the middle stage will depend on which of the three possible areas has been agreed in the beginning phase: losses, role transitions, or role disputes. With losses the therapist will help the patient describe in detail the actual death: what happened, whether it was expected or not, what the funeral was like, and any rituals involved. They will focus on any feelings, particularly when these were negative or ambivalent. Patients often need special help to think and talk about the loss and any associated difficult memories, about what they miss, and how to begin to move forward. For one patient this had become a seemingly overwhelming task, after the sudden death of her 'perfect' husband. He had been the one to take responsibility for comforting and supporting her in all aspects of life—practical, interpersonal, and emotional. Suddenly she was deprived of it all, with few psychological tools for managing the catastrophic fall-out. How could she even begin to admit to any angry or mixed feelings towards this paragon?

For role transitions, the therapy starts by identifying which spheres of life are affected. These can include work roles or social roles such as moving home or the children leaving, or they can be biological to do with health or ageing. What often matters most is whether the transition was planned, whether it was wanted or not, and whether it was accompanied by a loss of support. The therapist helps the patient recognize the feelings connected to the transition, particularly any sense of loss. The patient's capacities and resources are not neglected—both internal and external strengths are identified. Opportunities arising from the change are sought which might require learning new skills or managing new challenges. Learning how to assert needs and preferences, or even taking risks, can be part of this process.

A *communication analysis* often has a central place in role disputes *or* conflicts. This carefully explores what the patient wishes for, and whether it is reasonable and realistic. Time is spent understanding what she wants to say, how she says it, how this comes across to others, and whether it is understood by them. A withdrawn woman, used to taking a back seat in the family, thought resentfully that others should be able to 'read her mind'. She therefore failed to spell things out, or else she tended to say things in such a soft voice that they didn't hear it or take it seriously. The therapist will help the patient make potential links with symptoms. Any mismatch between what the person had aimed for and the actual interpersonal outcome is carefully discussed. Different ways of communicating can be explored by brainstorming or role plays, always encouraging the patient to come up with ideas herself and try them out. Although IPT does not use homework as such, the patient might be encouraged to rehearse and practise things between sessions.

The end phase of therapy focuses on reviewing and consolidating any gains, and if necessary making contingency plans for the future. As the ending is a transition in itself, some of the skills learned earlier can be applied to it.

Time-limited psychotherapy

As with most therapies, the initial model has been refined by experience and research. Dynamic Interpersonal Therapy or DIT is a recent such development in the UK, which lasts for sixteen sessions. It is an approach to IPT which combines an interpersonal focus with a more psychoanalytic stance, following a clear manual through the different stages of therapy. It uses interpretations of unconscious feelings and reactions in combination with what is known as *mentalization*. This comprises techniques to enhance the patient's capacity to reflect on her own states of mind, and through this to better understand what others might be feeling or thinking. By becoming more aware in this way she can improve her ability to understand and manage relationships.

Cognitive analytic therapy (CAT)

CAT was first developed in the 1980s in the UK by Dr Anthony Ryle, a general practitioner working with students in a university setting and later in adult mental health services. His initial aim was to create a *common language* for the psychotherapies. He was frustrated with psychoanalysis for its resistance to research, and with behaviour therapy for its reductionism. CAT takes psychiatric diagnoses and individual presenting problems seriously, but quickly moves to address the difficulties behind them. It focuses on the sense of self, often negative or fragmented, which is trapped by unhelpful relationship patterns.

CAT is a time-limited therapy, usually sixteen weekly sessions with one follow-up at three months. For more complex difficulties, this can be extended to twenty-four sessions with additional follow-ups. Like most brief therapies, CAT is an interactive model, based on collaboration and joint exploration. The model shares the analytical interest in exploring the early roots of interpersonal difficulties and the need for all of us to have a sense of our own story or narrative. It tries to understand how we have arrived at this point in our lives and what keeps us here, even—or especially—when the personal cost is high.

A joint *reformulation* of the patient's narrative, and the core patterns emerging from it, is expressed in the form of a letter, derived from the discussions in the first few sessions. This is initially brought in draft form, written by the therapist, and read out aloud by her. A common reaction to hearing the letter is a sense of being validated, as if troubles have been witnessed or acknowledged. The letter summarizes the person's life experiences and lays out the conclusions she has drawn from them. These conclusions are usually about her sense of personal value, about her relationships and how to deal with feelings and conflicts that emerge within them. The patient takes the draft letter away, rereads it, and brings it back with any amendments necessary to truly reflect their experiences. Once agreed, it becomes a shared basis for the remainder of the therapy and, indeed, for beyond therapy. Both parties can refer back to it at any time, and it helps them keep on track as therapy progresses. One patient took to keeping it in her bedside table and would read it to herself during times of stress, or to remind herself of how to act and think differently when falling back into old coping strategies.

A second function of the letter is to jointly identify a couple of main or *target* problems to focus the therapy on, plus unhelpful patterns or *procedures* stemming from attempts to solve these problems. Such procedures often end up as problems in their own right. A young woman brought back her letter with big, dirty footprints all over it, after leaving it on the staircase in her shared house. This spoke volumes of her tendency to let people 'walk all over her', while she attempted to fit in with everyone, in order to feel accepted and valued.

The main part of the therapy then involves exploring and understanding the various ways in which such unhelpful interpersonal patterns (known in CAT as *reciprocal roles*) manifest themselves. It includes paying attention to how the person treats herself, whether through self-neglect or overindulgence, or in more extreme self-harming ways. It will especially note when these patterns repeat themselves in the therapy relationship.

The patient and therapist together then look for *exits* or alternative ways of *self-management* and of interacting with others, and will use the therapy relationship or transference in this process. Change moments often come when a familiar interpersonal pattern is reactivated in a session, but accompanied by a new way of being or relating. This challenges the person's familiar expectations and habits. A common example is to expect rejection or criticism after having been angry with the therapist in a session or after revealing what were believed to be shameful secrets.

The main difference from IPT lies in the way these patterns are outlined very explicitly in CAT, especially in the form of a diagram, which the therapist and patient draw up together (see Figure 8). This identifies the interpersonal patterns that most commonly occur in the patient's life, including how these are linked. Such a visual representation helps her take a step back from the overall picture and develop what is called an *observing eye* (or 'I'), aiming for a more integrated sense of self. With this overview she can start to join up the dots, see a fuller picture, and get a different perspective on herself. The diagram can also help the person recognize patterns or *voices* that have been handed down through the generations and help them find their own, authentic voice through dialogue with the therapist.

The diagram uses the person's own words as much as possible, and the therapist will take care to build on their strengths and 'push where it moves'. The aim is to enhance the patient's (self-)reflective capacity and to gradually make the tools for this her own. Anthony Ryle wrote, 'what the person can do with the therapist today, s/he will do on her own tomorrow'. As with CBT, the patient is helped to become aware of their thought and behaviour patterns and to devise homework tasks. These usually involve small steps to break unhelpful patterns such as beginning to say no to others or creating time for self-care.

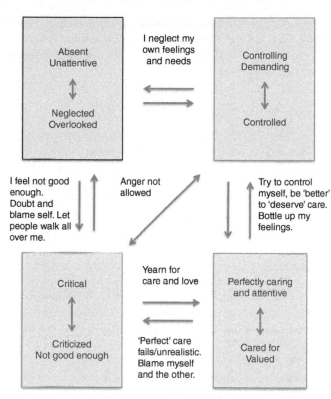

8. With the help of this CAT diagram the patient could see how her attempts to feel better about herself just led back to old, unhelpful patterns

Difficulties may emerge towards the end of therapy, often relating to past losses or unresolved separations. These will have been identified and anticipated in the early letter or in the diagram, which helps to address reactions to the ending, such as anger or sadness. The ending is also attended to by the patient and therapist each writing a goodbye letter. This is a letter to the other person, but also an opportunity to summarize the therapy. It covers what has been gained and learned, but also openly acknowledges missed opportunities, and realistically predicts challenges ahead. It is a chance to say a 'fare well' or an explicit 'goodbye', rather than repeat painful 'byes' of the past.

Solution-focused therapy (SFT)

SFT has links with Ericksonian thinking, and was developed by Steve de Shazer in the US during the 1970s. He noticed that clients seemed more energized when talking about solutions to their problems and how they would like their future to be, rather than analysing past difficulties. A central feature of the model is its *non-pathologizing stance*. It identifies healthy aspects of the person's experience that can be used, and it underscores that they already have resources to draw on. Therapy becomes a process of mobilizing and building on these to resolve problems, always with an eye to the future. A refreshing change if you have felt mired in problems for a long time! The focus in SFT is on 'competences rather than deficits, strengths rather than weaknesses, possibilities rather than limitations'. SFT can be very brief, often just three to six sessions.

SFT seeks solutions which 'fit the client rather than the problem'. In this it is very like IPT and CAT, but it is more explicitly directed towards solutions for the future rather than linking with the past. SFT uses a number of specialized techniques referred to as *skeleton keys*. One is inviting people to become aware of *exceptions*, times when they succeeded in solving their problems. It also involves identifying and mobilizing the client's personal and social resources, and imagining how they would like their future to be. This might include asking the *miracle question* discussed below, but mainly uses small, manageable steps when trying to change.

Personally relevant and realistic goals are generated. These are very concrete and require specific actions, rather than being vague formulations expressed in negative terms, such as wanting 'not to feel depressed any more'. The aim is for 'good enough' or satisfactory outcomes, with agreed ways of recognizing when these are achieved. Links are made between outcomes and what clients have done differently, so that they can take credit for their own achievements. Problems are discussed openly, with the therapist taking their share of responsibility. The therapist might ask questions such as 'What have I missed?' or 'What needs to happen today?'

SFT pays very close attention to the use of language. Questions are usually framed positively: 'What are your best hopes for this session?' 'What are you already doing that is helpful?' 'How will you know that today has been helpful?' This engages the person in examining their expectations and their own role in changing. Questions cover how the person will know when things are getting better or how many sessions are needed.

The miracle question, a striking SFT technique, goes something like this:

> Imagine that while you are asleep tonight a miracle occurs, and when you wake the problem you have told me about has disappeared. You are now problem free. However, because you have been asleep you won't know that the miracle has happened. What will you notice when you wake up that shows you things are different?

You are encouraged to ask yourself about the experience, again using positive language: 'What will I be doing differently?' 'What will I be saying?' 'How will it affect my life?' 'How would I know that?' 'What will others notice and how will they describe it and react?' 'What else will be different?' 'And what else…? And what else…?'

An angry young student regularly sabotaged himself by missing course deadlines, getting into drunken fights, and generally underperforming, rather than stand up to his father and challenge what he saw as high family expectations. Via the 'miracle' he might allow himself to enjoy doing well. The therapy focuses on how this will manifest itself, not on wishful thinking. What will the person be doing and thinking differently, and what are they doing now that will move them towards this 'miracle' scenario? So our student might identify how he was speaking more openly to his parents, that he was getting support from his brother in this, that he had cut down on his drinking, and that it had made a difference to his girlfriend.

SFT therapy sessions use *scaling*. So in relation to the miracle question the therapist might say: 'If on a scale of 1 to 10, 10 means you have already got there, and 0 means you haven't even started, where would you say you are today?' If the young man thinks that he is on a 3, he might review with the therapist what he did to get there, and what he needs to do to get to point 4 before next week. Scaling can be used at any time during or between sessions. One can rate where one was before, what one did to get from there to here, what are realistic hopes, what might sabotage change, and how to prevent this. SFT always uses positive questions, such as 'What makes me hopeful that I will move up the extra two points?'

Much of the work in SFT takes place between sessions using *tasking* or homework assignments. These involve thinking about the change you desire and the actions needed to achieve it. It means trying out and practising new skills independently and in the contexts where they belong. Some homework simply involves observational tasks, such as noticing things that already work well or keeping notes of positive changes. These can then be combined with behavioural tasks—doing things differently, such as saying no rather than giving in. Similarly, cognitive tasks will provide alternatives to negative thinking habits, such as 'Today I didn't let my worry stop me from going to the shops on my own' rather than 'I will never get back to having an independent life'. Using rituals or metaphors that mark a new stage or symbolize the achievement of a task can boost morale and give a sense of achievement.

As in all time-limited or brief therapies, the ending of therapy will have been on the agenda right from the start. SFT differentiates explicitly between treatment goals and life goals. Without this any therapy can become overextended, invite dependency, and unwittingly undermine the self-confidence and self-reliance that has been built up. Unlike in CAT, SFT clients will determine when therapy should end, and SFT therapists find that most opt for a brief input. The 'good enough' outcome between 'miracle' and the status quo is identified early, and anticipated in detail, including how it will be recognized if and when it is achieved. It is then time to stop.

What these and other brief or time-limited therapies share is the sense that because time is at a premium, every session counts. Both parties have to make active use of the time available to them. A focus is created at a very early stage, and the patient or client plays an active role in addressing their difficulties, both within and between sessions. There is also an unspoken belief that once people begin to do things differently, those around them will respond differently, and therefore much of the working through will occur naturally within these relationships. Obstacles in this process can be anticipated in the therapy, and new alternatives practised. In this way, the therapy quickly starts to look towards the future and draws on the person's own resources. This in itself reduces the risk of dependency with its potential to undermine confidence, and represents one of the major advantages of time-limited psychotherapy.

Chapter 5
Counselling

Many more of us will see a counsellor than ever be treated by a psychotherapist. Family doctor surgeries, colleges and schools, and many workplaces now employ counsellors. How is counselling different from psychotherapy? The word has several meanings—from a careers counsellor who advises on jobs, to being 'counselled' (told off) about work performance. In this book counselling refers to a confidential relationship between a client (the term preferred by counsellors, rather than patient) and an individual who is trained to listen attentively and who will try and help you improve things through support and understanding. What is the difference, then, between counselling and psychotherapy? This is a good question, but one that is not easy to answer. The boundaries are blurred and no definition pleases everyone. However, there are some recognizable and useful differences.

Overall, counselling is less formal than psychotherapy, and the relationship between counsellor and client more equal. The word counselling itself is a bit less 'threatening' and therapists working in schools or colleges are often referred to as counsellors to reduce anxiety about going to see them. Counselling also tends to be shorter, often just half a dozen sessions. It is rarely more than once a week and is usually less expensive. Most counselling training focuses predominantly on the use of counselling skills and on building the therapeutic relationship rather than on any complex model of mental functioning. It is generally less theory-laden. This does not mean there are no guiding principle, or that counsellors make it up as they go along, but you are unlikely to have a sense that a specific interpretation of your problems is imposed on you or on the process. As with psychotherapy, counselling can focus on specific symptoms or on more general problems of living. There are times when counselling is preferable to more formal psychotherapies, as in coping with acute and overwhelming events such as a bereavement or a relationship break-up.

Initially there was no training requirement for counsellors. Individuals with a wide experience of human life and with a warm and tolerant personality simply 'became' counsellors. Although still very variable in length and intensity, training requirements are becoming more formalized. Many counsellors in the UK are registered with the British Association of Counselling and Psychotherapy (BACP), although they are not required to be. To be registered they need to have completed a recognized training course, many of which require them to have spent some time in counselling themselves. They must have a supervisor with whom to discuss practice and keep up to date with their subject. The BACP was originally the British Association of Counselling, but it added Psychotherapy in 2000 as counselling training became more sophisticated. The name in itself is emblematic of the overlap between counselling and psychotherapy, which we have outlined. Let us start with the fundamentals of counselling practice, before describing some approaches in more detail.

Rogerian or client-centred counselling

Whatever they are called (existential, rational emotive, problem-based) most counselling draws on the core tenets of Carl Rogers' client-centred approach. Carl Rogers (1902–1987) was an American psychologist and psychotherapist who reacted against the pessimistic view of human nature that dominated psychotherapy during his training. He rejected its excessive focus on symptoms and disorders, basing his approach on *humanism* and *existentialism*. Humanism emphasizes the basic goodness and positive striving of all individuals, while existentialism teaches that the meaning of our lives lies in what we do with them. To be what he called *fully functioning* we continually have to make choices, and making choices is inherently stressful. Rogers concluded that the only one who could know what was right for an individual was that person himself. In client-centred counselling, the client is always the real expert whose judgement should be trusted when things are unclear.

The titles of Rogers' most influential books (*On Becoming a Person* and *A Way of Being*) demonstrate his outlook and underscore his fundamental principle of counselling. Counsellors have to embody the counselling process; it is not a technique to be learned but a philosophy to be embraced and lived. Counsellors must accept the basic value and goodness of everyone (including themselves) and recognize the healing power of self-awareness and human relationships in the conduct of their daily lives. Without this their counselling would be a hollow sham. Rogerian counsellors disapprove of technique and explanations, relying instead on their style of relating and on clarification.

The core conditions

Rogers believed that certain core features of the counselling relationship were responsible for healing. Of the original conditions, he described three that have become accepted as the basis of all psychotherapies. Two of the others are so self-evident they are hardly mentioned. One of these is that there has to be a psychological contact, a *real* relationship, which fully engages both counsellor and client—one that they are both aware of. Counsellors allow a greater degree of self-disclosure, acknowledging the feelings in the room, and may sometimes share aspects of their own experience, such as a bereavement. In drug and alcohol counselling services an openly acknowledged history of addiction is often a requirement. The second 'self-evident' condition is to communicate this engagement and understanding to the client. It is no use having all this commitment if the client remains blissfully ignorant of it. What, then, are the three core conditions for successful counselling and psychotherapy?

Congruence or genuineness

This means that the counsellor is fully engaged both in himself and in the relationship. Rogers originally used 'congruence' to convey that the counsellor's personality matched (was 'congruent with') her behaviour in the session. She is not putting on a professional front, so can legitimately draw on her own experiences in the therapy. The declared aims of the counselling—those agreed by counsellor and client—then really are shared objectives. Congruence is now more often described as *genuineness* or *authenticity*. The three core conditions will vary in intensity over time, but genuineness is a precondition for the other two. A counsellor who denies that she is anxious in a session, while her body language clearly demonstrates she is, will find it hard to help a client to be honest.

Empathy

The counsellor has to gain an understanding of what the client is going through, emotionally as well as intellectually. Empathy means being able to *feel what* the other person is experiencing. It is not the same as sympathy, which is to *feel for* their plight. Accurate empathy is a core skill in all therapy. We need to be able to 'get under the skin' of our patients and to see the world through their eyes. Empathizing with a client means acquiring an 'as if' experience of what they are going through, not sharing it directly. The therapist does not have to be personally anguished to empathize—in fact this could be most unhelpful.

Establishing empathy often requires *clarifying* emotions. Rogerian counsellors frequently repeat the clients' comments (*mirroring*), often with a questioning tone to encourage them to tease out what exactly they are experiencing. What matters is that the client, not the counsellor, understands. This mirroring of the client's utterances has at times led to a cruel and dismissive caricature of Rogerian counselling, in which such repetition is presented as purely reflex:

> CLIENT: I feel awful.
> COUNSELLOR: You feel awful.
> CLIENT: It's hopeless. I'm going to end it all.
> COUNSELLOR: You feel hopeless. You're thinking of ending it all.
> CLIENT: I'm jumping out of the window!
> COUNSELLOR: You're jumping out of the window!

Of course it is not at all like this. Mirroring and clarification are active processes to deepen understanding, without which change cannot take place or freer and healthier choices be made.

Unconditional positive regard (respect)

It is difficult to imagine helping someone in counselling or psychotherapy if you actively dislike them. Rogers believed that you have to have a real desire for your client to do well, and to genuinely respect their struggle. At the very least you should not find yourself disapproving of them, and certainly not express such disapproval. This may seem a counsel of perfection, as we all have our prejudices. The need to believe in people's fundamental goodness does not mean that counsellors are always 'warm and cuddly'. The clarification employed to deepen empathy often requires asking hard questions and making uncomfortable observations.

Unconditional positive regard sounds very daunting so is now usually called *respect*. You can have a positive regard for someone despite finding some of their behaviour off-putting. Most therapists have strategies for maintaining this distinction, just as clergymen profess to 'love the sinner but hate the sin'. Counsellors who really cannot warm to a client may refer them on to a colleague, whereas a psychoanalyst is more likely to see such feelings as important counter-transference clues to be worked with.

As in the later psychotherapies, the relationship itself has a central importance in counselling. It is not simply a framework for exploring the patient's internal life, but a curative force in its own right. Many counsellors distrust theories and concepts such as the Oedipus complex, archetypes, or maladaptive schemas. The client is the only one who can answer the 'why', and remains the final expert.

However, the nature of the counselling relationship carries some specific risks. Because it is less structured and theory-bound, and because the training is usually shorter, things can go wrong. A naïve counsellor may blur professional boundaries too much and risk becoming overinvolved with their client, or become swept up in the suffering. Self-disclosure ('I recognize how this feels, my own brother died suddenly when I was young') can be very powerful, but it can also derail the treatment. It could overburden clients who may feel they then have to care for their counsellor. Regular supervision is necessary to manage this tricky balance, particularly if the counsellor has no other professional background (nurse, social worker, psychologist) where supervision is an established practice. The BACP has been at the forefront of developing codes of ethics and practice to address these risks. We will now describe some specific counselling approaches.

Existential therapy

Person-centred counselling derives its thinking in great part from existential philosophy. Existentialists believe that what matters is what we *do*, rather than who or what we *are*. It is our own actions (our *existence*) rather than some preconceived view of human nature (an *essence*) that is important. We constantly create our identity rather than being determined by it, and our lives are driven by *motives* rather than *causes*. Every choice we make defines us, and we have no option but to continually make choices. Existentialists emphasize that we are active agents in the world, not objects, so therapists strive strenuously to avoid *objectifying* or categorizing the patient. They emphasize a mutually interacting relationship, focused on the here-and-now and an immediate relationship with the world.

The American existentialist-humanistic approach

The first form of existential therapy was developed by Ludwig Binswanger in the 1930s and is now mainly of historical interest. The existentialist approach lives on in humanistic counselling and psychotherapy. Rollo May and his enormously influential pupil Irving Yalom shifted the focus to a consideration of the individual's subjective reality; that is, how the client experiences his own world. This deviates from the hard-line existentialist's insistent focus on interaction with the outside world. Their approach focuses back on to the client's inner life and emotions.

In contrast to Freud's rather dour pessimism, Yalom brings a sunny Californian positivity and optimism. He encourages the client to stay with their emotions and confront the defences they have erected to protect against life's complexity: 'feel the fear and carry on'. Like Rogers, Yalom encourages therapists to be open to the client, and he repeatedly insists that 'it is the relationship that heals'. Increased self-understanding may be helpful, but it is not enough, nor is it the crucial ingredient. The vital ingredient is the relationship itself.

This existential-humanistic approach re-engages with the unconscious, but it is warmer and more directive than psychodynamic counselling. It is concerned with the present and the future, rather than with the past.

Therapy focuses on four core existential concerns: death, freedom, isolation, and meaninglessness. Counselling approaches for the physically and even terminally ill have been extensively developed. Despite this apparently morbid preoccupation, the tone of existentialist-humanistic counselling is inexorably upbeat. Complaints of 'can't' are reframed as 'won't'. In his 1980 book *Existential Therapy*, Yalom exhorts the client to repeat regularly to himself or herself the following statements:

> Only I can change the world I have created
> There is no danger in change
> To get what I want I must change
> I have the power to change

The British existential school

In contrast to the sunny, Californian optimism of the American existentialist-humanists, the British existential therapy school assumes that 'life is an endless struggle'. Developed and popularized by the Dutch psychotherapist Emmy van Deurzen, this approach links back to traditional existentialism. It focuses on the immediate relationship with current reality rather than the intrapsychic, subjective world of the patient. It continues to emphasize the importance of an 'authentic' relationship, and rejects the trappings of formal psychotherapy and of diagnoses and classification. It construes patients' problems in terms of being 'clumsy at living'. True to its existentialist roots it is relentlessly descriptive rather than explanatory. The aim of therapy is to form a clearer awareness of experience rather than try to explain it. In this it takes from Rogerian therapy, and in practice it is very non-directive and democratic. It re-emphasizes 'being with the patient'. Its radical and anti-authoritarian (anti-expert) stance makes it very attractive to those who might have difficulty tolerating a more paternalistic or establishment approach.

Transactional analysis (TA)

TA is a very accessible theory of human interaction that is used by many integrative or eclectic counsellors. It was introduced in 1964 by Eric Berne in his bestselling book *Games People Play*. TA focuses on how we communicate with others, and it replaces the three familiar Freudian levels of super-ego, ego, and id with the mental states *parent*, *adult*, and *child*. Berne shared Rogers' and Yalom's broadly optimistic view of human nature and of our capacity to find success and happiness. Well-balanced individuals behave as adults and treat those around them as adults. This was captured in the title of one of the most successful TA books, *I'm OK, You're OK*.

Berne's approach achieved instant popularity, not only through his easily grasped structure of the parent, adult, and child roles, but via his description of a series of 'games' with catchy titles. The 'games people play' are based on the various permutations of the three roles (I act like a child that forces you to act as a parent, I act as a parent forcing you to respond as a child, and so on). Our tendency to fall into these roles in different situations will depend on our own issues (see Figure 9). We may feel driven to exploit

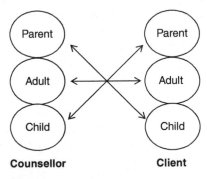

9. The three possible roles or 'ego-states'

the child role when we feel particularly insecure, or perhaps the parent role when we want to avoid the intimacy that can come from adult sharing.

The most famous of these games is the 'yes, but' gambit, which is very familiar not only to counsellors and therapists but surely to us all. The client describes a problem that is troubling her, but when the counsellor points to an obvious solution this is countered with an explanation of why it will not work:

> CLIENT: People dismiss me, even when they know I'm right, because I'm a scruffy dresser and they are all snobs.
>
> COUNSELLOR: What would it be like for you to ensure that when you are going to those sorts of meetings you put on a suit? You don't have to wear one all the time.
>
> CLIENT: If I weren't myself, if I had to put on a show, then it would all be a waste of time and I wouldn't care if they agreed.

On the face of it this is a reasonable adult-to-adult discussion about identity and integrity. However, the counsellor might note that the patient is using a victim-child state to engage the therapist's parent role. The conversations people engage in are built up of transactions which can be analysed in this way. The most complex transactions occur when there is a deliberate or unconscious difference between the overt social exchange (what is *said*) and the covert psychological intent (what is *meant*). These are referred to as *ulterior* transactions and need careful unpicking.

The most obvious strength of the TA approach is its common-sense quality. We can all grasp the three roles, and once the games are pointed out they are very easy to recognize. Counselling, of course, goes beyond simply 'spotting' games or the roles being used. It is the task of understanding *why* and *how* the client uses them with certain individuals and in specific circumstances that matters.

Drug and alcohol counselling

There is no recognized model for drug and alcohol counselling, but counselling is used extensively throughout such services. The practice is very widespread indeed, which should come as no surprise. It takes real commitment and energy to get off and to stay off drugs or alcohol—to 'kick the habit'. The initial phase of getting off drugs or alcohol under medical supervision is now fairly straightforward, but staying off is anything but. This is where counselling comes in. Staying off requires radical changes in lifestyle, giving up something that used to provide the pattern for your existence, moving away from a familiar social circle of other drinkers and addicts, with few other supports.

Alcoholics Anonymous (AA) is the most widespread system worldwide to support sobriety in alcoholics, and its offspring Narcotics Anonymous (NA) helps drug users stay 'clean'. Its *twelve steps approach* is not, in itself, a model of counselling but a structure, both social and psychological, to help the addict embark on a new life. AA insists that with no 'cure' for addiction, you have to renew a commitment to abstain 'one day at a time'. AA has quite a religious feel to it, with regular meetings where members ritually acknowledge their problems: 'My name is Janet and I am an alcoholic'.

Most services for addicted individuals go beyond supervised withdrawal and support from AA or NA meetings, and they also offer counselling. This aims to help the recovering addict understand the personal issues that may have driven them to drugs or alcohol and, just as importantly, those that keep them stuck in their habit. What emotional pain was the drug blunting? What failed relationships did the intoxication obscure? What made sobriety unbearable? In addiction circles the language is often quite dramatic: 'demons' rather than complexes, 'self-destruction' rather than risk-taking. But the issues are the same. Unresolved feelings, painful memories, low self-esteem, and disturbing ruminations make it harder to get off and stay off drink or drugs and to build new relationships.

As we have mentioned, there is no unique theoretical model of counselling for addictions—person-centred counselling is the most common approach. It often comes with strict rules on abstinence as a condition of attendance. Blunt confrontations are common, which can seem quite brutal to outsiders, although addicts often welcome them. They are only too familiar with their evasions and have extensive experience of 'fooling' previous counsellors. Many services insist that the counsellors are themselves recovered addicts who are familiar with such self-deception and so don't pull their punches when pointing it out.

Psychodynamic counselling

Distinguishing psychodynamic counselling from client-centred counselling is fairly easy, but distinguishing it from psychodynamic psychotherapy is not so straightforward. This is probably where the boundary between counselling and psychotherapy is the least clear. Many counsellors describe themselves as psychodynamic, so being clear what it is, and the difference between them, is worth some effort. While retaining many of the core features of counselling outlined at the beginning of this chapter, psychodynamic counsellors base their practice on traditional psychodynamic or psychoanalytic theory. They focus on helping the client become aware of unconscious conflicts and making sense of them, often using interpretations (see Chapter 2). The aim in psychodynamic counselling is 'to make the unconscious conscious'—Freud's 'where id was, ego shall be'. Once the client is properly aware of the unconscious forces shaping their experiences and behaviour, they can start to sort themselves out.

Psychodynamic counsellors are much more likely than client-centred counsellors to respond to a question with another question or an interpretation. Their aim is to uncover underlying issues. For instance, if a client comments that their counsellor looks under the weather, the Rogerian is likely to encourage them to explore in more detail their experience of that concern. The psychodynamic counsellor, however, may seek out underlying anxieties or hostilities: 'perhaps you think that the problems you have been sharing are too much for me and I am not coping?'

Psychodynamic counsellors pay particular attention to containing clients' distressing experiences, often rephrasing them so the client can confront them safely. The active emotional engagement buffers the pain of these experiences so that they can be carefully examined. This is often referred to as *holding*, a concept described by the analyst Donald Winnicott. It implies that the strength of the relationship is such that it can contain intense experiences that would otherwise be overwhelming.

By holding, and reflecting back a somewhat more manageable version of the client's conflicts, the counsellor provides the opportunity to find an alternative way forward. The experience itself is partly curative. The presence of a trained person who is able to withstand such stresses can be used to explore and replay old conflicts and find new solutions. Unlike most other counsellors, psychodynamic counsellors allow a degree of regression and for clients to become more dependent so that they can explore their more child-like feelings and impulses.

In practice, psychodynamic counselling can be quite long term—many months or even a year or two. It is also rather more formal, being strict about times and self-disclosure. The client is no longer the sole expert on their inner life, although clarifying it is very much a collaborative exercise.

Telephone counselling

The Samaritans in the UK and their sister organizations across the world have long demonstrated the value of fast access by telephone, and now often by e-mail, to a sympathetic listener. They provide an opportunity to express and share acute distress rather than simply soldiering on or resorting to drastic acts such as self-harm or suicide attempts. The telephone service Child Line in the UK offers similar opportunities to children who experience neglect or abuse. In our age of the Internet and Skype the lessons learned from these services have been taken on board by counsellors and psychotherapists. In very dispersed communities such as rural Australia it is now possible to have quite extensive tele-counselling or tele-psychotherapy.

The relationship between counselling and psychotherapy

The outline of the counselling approaches in this chapter demonstrates how complex the relationship is between counselling and psychotherapy. Counselling is not just some watered down or cheap alternative to psychotherapy. From Rogers on it has forged its own theoretically coherent and individual path. While it has learned from the more established psychotherapies, we have also highlighted some of its own unique contributions. These arose out of its more equal relationship and more obviously shared experience. In turn these insights have fed back into the practice of the formal therapies. Perhaps more importantly, it has made a supportive space for self-reflection a realistic proposition for the majority of us.

Chapter 6
Cognitive behaviour therapy

CBT is *very* different to the other therapies covered in this book, so this chapter is also going to be different. Like the therapy itself it will have lots of structure and lots of lists. CBT emphasizes *thinking* and *thoughts*. The underlying premise is that 'faulty' thinking gives rise to anxiety and depression rather than the other way round. CBT is the product of bringing together the strengths of behaviour therapy and those of cognitive therapy.

Behaviour therapy is exactly what the name implies. It was a radical departure from psychoanalysis with its emphasis on unconscious motivation and symbolization, and it simply tried to help the patient alter their behaviour. It is ultimately derived from the work of the Russian psychologist Pavlov and his experiments with his dogs. Pavlov discovered how behaviours could be 'conditioned' by associating them with stimuli, such as making his dogs salivate at the sound of a bell after getting them used to the bell being rung before food was delivered (see Figure 10).

The most famous (or perhaps infamous) exponent of this learning theory was B. F. Skinner, who believed that all behaviours were learned by this process of association. Skinner invented a special cage for rats which became known as a 'Skinner box'. In this they were either rewarded with food or punished with electrical shocks when they performed specific actions, and they demonstrated

"And then it hit me: I'm salivating over a goddam bell."

10. Behaviour therapy derives from learning theory and the conditioned reflexes that Pavlov noticed when his dogs associated the bell before feeding with the food itself

remarkably quick learning. His conclusion was that any behaviour, whether in a rat or a human, could be trained by 'reinforcing' it with positive stimuli (rewards), or extinguished by associating it with negative stimuli (an unpleasant taste, a small electric shock). In clinical practice relaxation was most often used as the positive stimulus to enable patients to confront feared situations, usually in a stepwise manner. Behaviour therapy is particularly successful in phobias (simple phobias such as fear of spiders and also in more complex phobias such as agoraphobia) and in sexual therapies. 'Aversive' behaviour therapy, where unwelcome behaviours are associated with unpleasant stimuli (e.g. alcohol with a nausea-inducing drug), has been less influential.

Behaviour therapies are nowadays more likely to be considered as a routine treatment rather than as a psychotherapy. It is a fine distinction and one can argue both ways. However, they do generally lack the specific, highly personal relationships we associate with psychotherapy, so will not be dealt with in any detail in this book. However, that is not to dismiss them. They still play an important role in child psychiatry and in some services for individuals with learning disabilities.

Cognitive therapy was developed in the 1960s by Aaron Beck in America. He was struggling to help some of his patients who did not respond well to his analysis. They appeared to value self-mastery much more than self-understanding: *control* of their symptoms rather than understanding or insight. 'Cognition' is usually defined as the mental process of acquiring knowledge and understanding through thought, experience, and the senses. The focus in cognitive therapy is therefore on our patterns of thinking and 'knowing' things, which is often based on unquestioned assumptions. Beck's change of focus provided a radical shift, which eventually led to the development of CBT.

The underlying philosophy of CBT was propounded by the Ancient Greek philosophers, the Stoics. They believed that happiness depends not on what happens to us but on what we make of it. We call a Stoic someone who seems able to shrug off life's misfortunes and still remain contented and productive. So CBT does not dwell on the difficulties of your childhood or subsequent traumas, but on what you have made of them and how you are coping now. It focuses on the present. It insists that you are in charge and can make choices, and it is overwhelmingly interested in what you think.

CBT therapists are not naïve about this focus on thinking. They know that thinking, feeling, and behaviour (indeed even physical health) are all interconnected and continually influence each other. There are constant feedback loops between them. However, CBT emphasizes how thinking drives emotions, and it selects thinking as the point in the system where change can most effectively be achieved. Sessions are consequently very different from most other therapies, but before describing that practice it helps to understand some of the theory.

Here comes the first list of three. CBT theory identifies three layers of thinking to address (see Box 2). The first is *negative automatic thoughts*, below this our *underlying assumptions*, and then at the very fundamental level our *core beliefs* often called *schemas*. Most CBT will concentrate on negative automatic thoughts and only dive deeper during more complex and protracted therapies.

Negative automatic thoughts

We are continually making judgements about what is going on around us. We know from cognitive neuroscience that the vast majority of these judgements are instantaneous and unconscious. We respond accurately to our environment without being aware of the cues we receive, or of the assumptions about them that condition our responses. In a crowded bar we move away from someone staggering without even noticing we are doing it, never mind being aware of why. We have registered subconsciously that they may be drunk, and we know from long experience to be wary of intoxicated people. We make such judgements and assumptions all the time, instantaneously, without being aware of them. We have to, there are too many to be made. Were we to consider them all consciously we would be completely paralysed by indecision.

When we are stressed our assumptions can become more rigid and negative—we easily assume the worst. We are unaware of this happening but it affects what we do, and soon also how we feel, so we may become anxious or depressed and not be sure why. We are unaware of how such automatic thoughts can cause and maintain anxiety and depression.

CBT aims to help us identify and then challenge these negative automatic thoughts. The processes used are called *Socratic questioning* and *collaborative empiricism*. Essentially it starts with a simple question: 'What is going through your mind right now?' Clarifying and challenging thoughts, collaborative empiricism, involves three further questions:

1. Is there any evidence for this thought?
2. Are there other ways to understand what is happening?
3. What are the implications of thinking this way?

Underlying assumptions

These assumptions shape the way we understand how the world works. They are the maxims, or principles, we apply in managing our everyday lives. They state a consequence to an action, which we believe to be inevitable. '*If* I do this *then* this will happen.' 'I *should* do this *because…*' '*Unless* I do this *then…*' 'I *must* do this *or…*' These assumptions underlie the negative automatic thoughts, and Beck highlighted three that he regularly encountered:

I am nothing unless I am loved—*acceptance*
I am what I accomplish—*competence*
I cannot ask for help—*control*

Core beliefs (schemas)

These are the fundamental beliefs we hold about ourselves, which shape who we feel we are. They are often paired so that

> **Box 3 The CBT rule of three**
>
> 1. Beliefs about ourselves
>
> 2. Beliefs about others
>
> 3. Beliefs about the world

for each important belief we also hold its mirror opposite in balance. When stressed we all too easily lose sight of our positive self-belief and focus on its opposite. A successful professional may for example usually think of herself as hard working and reliable. However, under pressure she switches to believing she is a fraud who gets by on the absolute minimum and will be found out. We don't have core beliefs about every tiny detail of our lives, only those aspects that are important to us. Again there is a CBT rule of three (see Box 3).

Only in very protracted (schema-based) CBT are core beliefs addressed directly. Therapists usually rely on the work on negative automatic thoughts to influence negative core beliefs.

CBT practice

The immediately striking thing about CBT is that it is *short*, sometimes very short. Beck recommended between four and fourteen weekly sessions for anxiety states, although most therapies hover between six and twenty sessions. You also usually know exactly how long it is going to take right from the start. Many services are very strict about how many sessions are offered. The IAPT service (see Chapter 5) offers four to six sessions.

CBT is very structured and pretty prescriptive. Therapists are taught in great detail about its specific procedures and individual components. They may even use a manual outlining them, sometimes giving the order in which they should be applied. CBT therapists consider this open and transparent approach to be an important strength of their model. There is no mystique, and patients are encouraged to read up about the various practices. Being well-informed improves collaboration and reduces misunderstandings.

Socratic dialogue

Socrates was a Greek philosopher whose teaching consisted of asking questions (see Figure 11). He believed that we already know the answers we seek but need help in finding them. This process came to be known as Socratic dialogue. You are the one who has the automatic thoughts and only you can identify them (think back to Carl Rogers' client-centred approach in Chapter 5).

11. Socrates was a Greek philosopher known to us through the writings of Plato. Socrates was so influential that he was condemned to death by drinking hemlock for 'corrupting the minds of the youth of Athens' by his teaching. His method used probing questioning to bring out knowledge

The therapist's function is to help you do this using careful questioning. She will insist on clarity, especially in distinguishing thinking from feeling. It is remarkable how often we say 'I feel' when we mean 'I think'. If we say 'I feel that the banking crisis is now resolving' we hardly register that what we mean is we *think* the banking crisis is now resolving. We may also have feelings about it, perhaps relief or anger that it was allowed to happen, but that is a different matter from our thoughts.

There are many techniques for identifying and clarifying automatic thoughts. Insisting that patients answer with statements rather than hypotheses is important in the early stages:

THERAPIST: What were you thinking just then?

CLIENT: It was probably something about how my wife would react to my leaving my job.

THERAPIST: That's a speculation about what you *might* have been thinking, what was the exact thought?

CLIENT: OK, I thought she would consider me stupid and impulsive.

Asking patients to describe the worst potential outcomes from their current train of thought is also used:

What's the worst thing you think would happen if your wife thought you were being impulsive? Do you think she would despise you or perhaps even leave you?

Getting patients to recall distressing recent events (*imagery*) also sharpens awareness of the associated thoughts. Sometimes the therapist may be fairly sure what the patient is thinking, because they have come across it in many previous patients. In CBT the therapist can suggest this as a possibility (although not a certainty)—something that other therapists might be very reluctant to do.

Collaborative empiricism

Once negative automatic thoughts have been identified they need to be tested and examined. This is referred to as *collaborative empiricism*. It is called empirical because it tests ideas in practice rather than in theory, and collaborative because therapist and patient do it together. For example, a patient reports a setback: 'It was disastrous, a hopelessly public screw-up. Nobody will ever take my opinions seriously again.' The therapist encourages him to think through the evidence for and against this belief. She may ask him to give examples of when his opinion has been ignored and when it has not. The patient is encouraged to find examples of how people have recently followed his advice and taken him seriously. Collecting such evidence can demonstrate that the negative automatic thought is grossly exaggerated, if not downright wrong. *Catastrophizing* is a common feature in automatic thinking. There may indeed have been a price paid for some mistake, but it does not mean everything is lost, despite how it may feel. Introducing shades of grey into such black-and-white thinking characterizes collaborative empiricism.

The distinction between identifying and testing automatic thoughts can be less clear in practice. An example is getting patients to think through the pros and cons of individual thoughts and defining the terms they use more clearly. Doing this both refines and simultaneously tests these thoughts. Patients often apply more severe standards to their own behaviour than to that of others. This can be exposed by asking them to apply what they have just said about themselves to others: 'Would you judge your wife that way?' 'Would you bring up your children to believe that?'

In all CBT exercises thoughts are treated as hypotheses to be tested, not incontrovertible facts. Testing them in the session can demonstrate this, but the most powerful test is to try them out in reality. Such *behavioural experiments* are part and parcel of CBT.

They will be considered more in the next section about homework, which is where they are usually conducted.

Collaborative empiricism has two functions. The first, and most obvious, is to identify, test, and modify negative automatic thoughts. The second is to teach the patient to become his own therapist. The process of questioning matters as much as the answers. Learning to recognize and test dysfunctional thoughts and internalizing this process is held to be responsible for CBT's long-term effects. You are no longer a passive victim of your thinking.

Homework

With so few sessions it is important to make every one count. In dynamic psychotherapy holding on to an emotion or thought until the next session can be important learning in itself, but CBT therapists don't want patients to keep things on hold for a week. They want them to work on what they are learning, to practise and test it out between sessions. Therapists encourage clients to keep putting into practice what they learn in sessions and so devise homework tasks. The end of each session is used to review what has been learned and to plan together how to practise it before the next session. Most homework consists of deliberately trying out feared actions to learn their real consequences, but there is a whole range of possible tasks.

Many *cognitive* homework tasks are things you can do alone. One is simply to read and learn more about your problems and the possible treatments. CBT therapists strongly encourage self-education and may suggest chapters from specific books, especially CBT self-help books. Another is writing, usually writing a *daily thought record*. This records the occurrence of negative automatic thoughts, noting their context and perhaps how you challenged them. Listening again to tape-recorded sessions is particularly useful, as it isn't always easy to take in everything during a session. Remembering upsetting events in great detail, visualizing them happening (imagery), can feed back into the next session. Listening to recorded sessions or writing down your thoughts also helps get over the shyness of early psychotherapy.

Behavioural homework is generally the more powerful challenge. After all, this is real empiricism—testing out what happens in the real world, not in your imagination. *Behavioural experiments* test out individual automatic thoughts. Imagine you have identified a powerful negative automatic thought during a session: 'Any doubt I express indicates incompetence and people at work will despise me.' You then find some situations at work to practise saying 'I'm really not sure what is best here', and observe (and then write down) what the response is. Most likely it is something like: 'Yes, I know, it is a tricky one. I'm never entirely sure myself.' This experience is much more powerful than just imagining it. Often one has to work up to such experiments one step at a time. Confidence improves with each success. *Activity scheduling* in depression can act in the same way, as completing small, defined tasks chips away at the belief that they 'can't do anything at all'.

CBT homework is agreed between patient and therapist. It is not like school where the teacher sets the same homework for the whole class. CBT homework, especially behavioural experiments, has to be very specific. It must cover the where, when, and how, not just the what. It is specific to the issues under examination and is negotiated and usually written down. Often the tasks are practised in the session: 'OK, we have agreed on what you are going to say at work, try it out on me first.' The homework experiences are reviewed in the following session.

The structure of CBT sessions

So far we have focused on the content of CBT sessions, but CBT has a well-developed structure which is also important for its success. CBT therapists always start with a careful formulation of your problems in the assessment session. As with everything else in CBT there is nothing secret about it and your therapist will share it with you. Because CBT is brief, the formulation must include an agreement on what will be worked on. The formulation takes account of the past, but in shorter, simpler CBT therapies past experiences take a back seat to what is going on now. In more extensive therapies for complex problems understanding the past may be crucial to properly understanding current concerns, and the formulation will take account of this. If there are more problems than can be addressed in the time available, the formulation will prioritize them.

Individual sessions are also structured. They start with a *review* of the previous session and any homework. An *agenda* is set for the session, agreeing what will be worked on. Towards the end of the session what has gone on will be *reviewed* and *summarized*. Homework for the upcoming week will be negotiated and agreed. All this sounds businesslike and very hard work, but as with all therapies the CBT therapist is closely attuned to how the patient is feeling. Also, as with everything in CBT, these are joint decisions and not simply imposed on you.

All therapies aim to bring lasting change. CBT helps you to learn the techniques that make you your own therapist, so that you can continue practising what you have learned. Having one or more 'booster' sessions after the therapy ends is common, sometimes the final sessions are spaced out with longer intervals between them. Negative thoughts are not abolished by CBT—we all have them. However, CBT should make you much better at dealing with them. Some falling off of improvements is inevitable after almost any therapy, and CBT therapists warn patients that it will happen. A review session between a month and three months after finishing can serve to re-energize and fine tune the self-therapy. It also helps make the point that the work goes on long after the therapy ends.

CBT therapists rely heavily on measurement. They use questionnaires in their work to measure symptoms and track changes. These include scales for specific disorders (obsessive compulsive disorder, eating disorders, etc.), but anxiety and depression ratings are the ones most widely used. Scales are generally completed at the start and again at the end of therapy, to assess the outcome, but sometimes they are used to track changes during treatment. Filling out such questionnaires is more often a useful exercise in itself, training the patients to make judgements about degrees rather than catastrophize.

The role of research

CBT has been notable among the psychotherapies in its wholehearted embrace of rigorous scientific testing of its effects. This follows logically from its approach. Just as the therapy tests the real effects of negative thoughts, so practitioners want to test the real effects of the treatment. CBT is the most scientifically investigated psychotherapy, with literally dozens of careful studies. Specific modifications for different disorders have also been tested, including CBT for eating disorders, for different anxiety disorders, personality difficulties, and sexual disorders.

CBT's engagement with research reflects its underlying empirical approach, but is also due to mainly being championed by clinical psychologists who have a very scientific training. One result is that in many publicly funded services it may be the only psychotherapy available. This is a pity, and doubly so. First because the evidence for non-CBT therapies does suggest that they are also effective, although there are far fewer studies. Second, it is a pity because CBT does not suit everyone, nor does it always work. No therapy suits everyone. Drop out rates are quite high in CBT, so where are these patients to look for further help? CBT's overwhelming lead in research is somewhat demoralizing for non-CBT therapists. However, failing to conduct research is not really a long-term option in our modern, evidence-based world.

Specialized CBT

Because the different components in CBT practice are so well described, they can be mixed and matched to different clinical needs and can be 'branded' for them. This can involve relatively minor, but highly effective, changes in practice such as that developed for eating disorders. CBT-E as it is called (the E stands for enhanced, not eating) is used with patients suffering from both anorexia nervosa and bulimia. It lasts for twenty sessions, forty for underweight patients, and requires from the outset that the patient tries to eat regularly and that they be weighed at each session. It downplays the examination of automatic thoughts, focusing more on the responses to change in behaviour and weight. Neither the dietary diary nor taped sessions are used, as they have been found to encourage unhealthy rumination. This is an example of CBT adapted and shaped to a specific clinical problem, rather than a major departure in practice.

Mindfulness-based cognitive therapy (MBCT) and dialectical behaviour therapy (DBT) go well beyond adaptation and add a range of novel practices. While DBT is a very specialized and restricted treatment, MBCT is increasingly widespread and popular. It has been shown to be particularly effective in reducing the risk of further relapses in people who have had several episodes of depression.

Mindfulness draws on Buddhist ideas of 'being in the moment' and the practice of meditation. Patients reduce the impact of negative thoughts by developing *metacognition*—being able to create a distance from which to think about their thinking. In practice this means recognizing a negative automatic thought as just that: a thought that one has which one can either accept or reject. There is no obligation to respond to it, it is enough simply to note it. Using mindfulness techniques of being in the moment, devoid of past and future, produces a more serene, non-judgemental state.

Mindfulness training consists of eight weekly two-hour classes, with a one-day event halfway through. It prescribes guided meditation for extended periods between sessions and developing a mindfulness approach in all aspects of daily life.

DBT, although it includes mindfulness practices, is almost the polar opposite in tone. It was developed for very troubled people whose lives were in chaos and who often self-harmed. It is very intensive and quite forceful. Weekly individual CBT sessions target reducing self-harm and developing skills to minimize risk and stress. It is called 'dialectical' because it has two competing elements, mindfulness versus confrontation. The latter involves learning how to regulate powerful feelings and tolerate distress.

CBT has a very different feel and a different ethos to the other psychotherapy and counselling approaches we have covered so far. It is much more structured and predictable. Some patients react against what they experience as a rather mechanical quality, far removed from explorations of personal narrative and sense of self. Others, however, welcome this clarity and structure. Longer and more complex CBT treatments often concern themselves with relationships and blur the sharp distinctions from more dynamic approaches, particularly when applied by more senior practitioners. Be that as it may, CBT is a radical departure which has changed the face of psychotherapy. It is still a relatively young, vigorous, and expanding innovation, and a *Very Short Introduction* devoted entirely to the subject is soon to be published. It will be fascinating to see how CBT looks in ten to fifteen years' time.

Chapter 7
Family, group, and interactive therapies

We have described various individual therapy approaches in which the patient's or client's descriptions of relationship and interpersonal problems are explored. However, there are a number of therapies that work directly with these problems, not just through the patient's recall. Some, such as couples and family therapy, directly involve all the individuals affected. Group therapy offers direct opportunities for feedback in interactions with others, with constructive challenges in the here-and-now on how to go about things differently. There are also more interactive therapies such as art and music therapy, which can be provided either with groups or individuals. These particularly suit patients who are less clear about what their problems are, or who might struggle to express them verbally.

There are countless variations of these more active therapies. In this chapter we will describe the practice of systemic family therapy, couples therapy, and group therapy, which are now widely established. We will also briefly introduce the practice of psychodrama, art therapy, and music therapy.

Systemic family therapy

> Freud is all nonsense; the secret of neurosis is to be found in the family battle of wills to see who can refuse longest to help with the dishes.
>
> Julian Mitchell, quoted by Robin Skynner
> in *One Flesh, Separate Persons*

We are all born into 'the hands of others', the cradle of the family. Salvador Minuchin, an influential early family therapist, describes families like this:

> In all cultures, the family imprints its members with selfhood. Human experience of identity has two elements: a sense of belonging and a sense of being separate. The laboratory in which these ingredients are mixed and dispensed is the family, the matrix of identity.

Robin Skynner wrote that the best way to learn how to create a happy and healthy family was to have been born into one. That way we learn how to 'find satisfaction in harmonious relationship to one another'. Aware of the enormous creative potential of the family it is not surprising that, when it becomes disordered, it possesses an equal potential for destruction.

Family therapy is often used when the referred patient is a child or adolescent. Originally, family therapists perceived the child's disturbance more as a marker of a family disturbance, but this is no longer necessarily so. A referral for family therapy does not imply that the family is considered responsible for the patient's problems, more a recognition that severe emotional problems can, and do, involve everyone in the family. For example, the families of younger patients with anorexia nervosa are usually offered therapy, and this has been found to be helpful. Nobody really knows what causes an individual girl to become anorexic, but a severe, life-threatening illness in a young person is bound to disrupt any family. Few who work with anorexia nervosa believe that the family 'causes' anorexia, and the therapy is aimed at finding ways to cope with the disorder for all involved.

The same would apply when the identified patient is seen by an adult mental health team, whether dealing with the painful consequences of a psychotic disorder in a member of the family or when an 'adult child' has become 'stuck' at home.

When families are struggling to find a healthy balance, systemic family therapy offers them an opportunity to take a step back and think together. It provides a chance to review patterns that might have become fossilized and find ways to renegotiate and change them. Family therapy aims to understand and intervene in the whole relationship context, rather than just with the problems of the member initially identified as the patient. Freeing up patterns at an early stage can bring prompt relief for all involved. Such freeing up can also prevent family members being burdened with restrictive family 'scripts' or myths.

Family therapy aims to improve the family's capacity to communicate clearly and openly with one another, exposing it to new perspectives and ideas. It is not so preoccupied with specific solutions for specific problems—problems arise constantly in all families—but with changing the family's style of interacting and operating. Family dynamics are immensely powerful, so the therapy aims to channel this energy in a more healthy direction. Clarifying communication clears away obstructions to the developmental stages that all families have to go through, and so allows its members to grow and move on.

Family therapists are very active and use a number of tried and tested 'tools'. One is the *genogram* (see Figure 12). This is a family tree, usually drawn up at the beginning of therapy. It outlines diagrammatically all the family members and their relationships to each other, and usually covers the last three generations. This

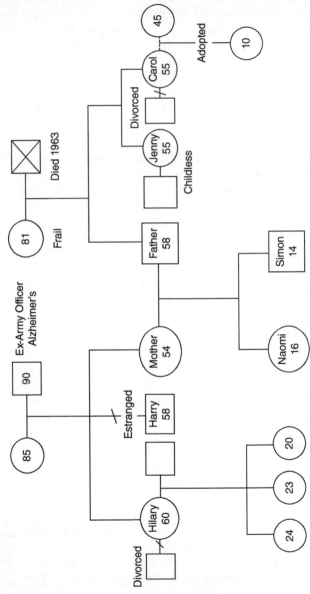

Psychotherapy

12. A family tree, or 'genogram', used in family therapy to demonstrate recurring family patterns. In this example we can see repeated broken relationships and also possible additional pressures on Simon as the only male offspring

helps the family see itself in context and with a wider perspective. Intergenerational patterns can emerge with startling clarity in this shared exercise.

Examining the genogram helps the family and the therapists to undertake what is called a *script analysis*. This is rarely done in a particularly formal manner, but involves working out the rules, spoken or more often unspoken, that govern how they relate. Four family 'scripts' are usually identified: the *circumstantial script* is what all the members know about their family history, and on which they base their overall behaviour; the *assumptive script* describes beliefs about, and emotional attitudes towards, their roles, both within the family and in the outside world; the *delivered script* is what they actually say to one another, the words they use to convey these assumptions; and finally the *subscript* is what we hold back from expressing, whether deliberately or not. This nevertheless continually affects our interactions, and all the more powerfully so for being unspoken.

In family and group therapies the participants are both *agents* and *observers*. So while the mother and her son Simon may be at loggerheads in a session over his recent truancy, the father and his sister Naomi observe how they constantly interrupt one another, ramping up the tension despite their best efforts to calm the situation down.

Collaborative team working is another striking feature of systemic family therapy, usually with two therapists working together. In some settings other members of the team may watch from behind a two-way mirror, even phoning in advice to the therapists! Obviously this only happens with the full agreement and consent of the family, and mainly in training settings. However, it demonstrates a remarkable break with psychotherapy's usual insistence on intimacy and confidentiality. So why does it happen? Family scripts can be inordinately powerful, with a whole set of well-entrenched routines devoted to keeping things as they are.

It takes intense, concerted effort for therapists to get into this system enough to obtain a good grasp of it. Yet they also have to remain something of an outsider to be able to 'shake it up' and create new experiences and a space to reflect. Conjoint work ensures that therapists can be both agents and observers. It also means that their working relationship can model more constructive and less defensive ways of interacting, such as when they ask each others' opinions or discuss their different experiences of what is going on.

Family therapists demonstrate a stance of neutrality by seeking out the views of each family member and taking them equally seriously. They often use a *circularity of enquiry*, turning to each member of the family individually as well as addressing the family as a whole. In the mother and son scenario outlined above, the therapists might try and loosen the stalemate as follows:

To FATHER: How do you think your wife feels when she's going on at Simon?

To SIMON: While you've been having these school problems, have you noticed any other changes in the family?

To NAOMI: What do you think happens to Simon when he has these rows with your mum?

To MOTHER: If this were a stage with characters in a play, where do you think Naomi feels herself to be at the moment?

To THE WHOLE FAMILY: What are things like for you as a family at the moment? How would you like it to be? What would you each need to do differently to get there? Who would be most likely to try it out?

Here we can see similarities with solution-focused therapy, and many aspects of family scripts have an overlap with the reciprocal roles of CAT (see Chapter 4). In common with most psychotherapy approaches, therapists aim to help *reframe* difficulties. Family therapists are known for their irreverence and tend to do this in a playful manner, where family members often find themselves laughing out loud. The aim is to show that rather than keep repeating 'more-of-the-same' sequences, things can be done differently, while not trying to achieve any 'right' way to do them.

Many things happen all at once in family therapy, and each member may have a different experience of it, so family therapists often write *therapeutic letters* in which they summarize what went on in the session. With the agreement of the family, these letters can also be a way of involving and communicating with other systems engaged with the family, such as school or a nursing team. This is particularly important as other professionals may inadvertently be maintaining or exacerbating a family's difficulties. Their responses, while entirely well-intentioned, may get in the way of change. A school nurse trying to support Simon by allowing him off lessons might need to understand that him telling his mother each evening that he had been in the sick bay was getting in the way of them getting to the root of their difficulties. Systemic work sometimes involves bringing more distant family members or other professionals into the sessions.

Couples therapy

Couples and marital therapy are more commonly available than family therapy. RELATE (previously called the Marriage Guidance Council) is best known in the UK for this, but almost all countries have similar organizations. The approach is very similar to family therapy, although it is not so common to have two therapists. Where there are, they are usually one man and one woman, and their collaboration in the sessions acts as a potent modelling experience.

Problems in relationships can have their roots in difficulties each partner may have had earlier in their lives. Institutions such as the Tavistock Centre in London employ a psychodynamic approach to understanding how this impacts on the couple in the present, but couples therapy usually restricts itself to altering the style of communication and focuses more on the present and the future. Couples, like families, have no shortage of grievances about each other, and the therapy has to get beyond the 'blame game'. The therapy often uses homework exercises—'get a babysitter, go out to somewhere you like, just the two of you'—to review in the next session. Sometimes prescribing what *not* to do is more important: 'talk for an hour planning a holiday together *without* mentioning the last two disasters'. This approach is used extensively in sex therapy, where prohibiting intercourse for a set period can remove inhibiting performance anxiety or prevent tensions building up. This can free up the warmth and intimacy that is needed for eventually making love and enjoying it.

Group therapy

As its name implies, group therapy involves several people together. Unlike family therapy these individuals do not generally know each other before coming to the group. Groups usually consist of between six and eight members plus the therapist (two co-therapists is quite common). They meet in the same place at the same time, usually for about ninety minutes once a week. The emphasis is on what goes on in the group, and members are asked not to meet outside. If they do meet (which almost invariably happens), they should be sure to report it back.

Group therapy is traditionally composed of individuals with a range of problems—anxiety, depression, phobias, relationship difficulties, etc. This range of problems and individuals (men and women, different ages, varying life experiences) makes the group a microcosm of ordinary life. It means that the full range of possible difficulties and conflicts is likely to occur in the group over time.

Therapists have to balance the diversity needed to provide a rich experience with ensuring that the group members have enough in common to gel. It is particularly important not to have one or two members who are clearly outliers. You don't want a single retired member in a group of twenty-year-olds, or someone with a dramatically different level of education or income to the rest of the group. It should be a spread of life-experience, not a random hotchpotch.

Not all groups are drawn from such a diverse population. Groups are also used extensively for individuals who share a similar problem such as eating disorders, addiction, or depression. Their advantage is that they can learn about different ways of coping. They are very supportive, as members realize they are not alone with their difficulties and can identify with each other's struggles. They can also be challenging, as members will know all the tricks and be able to confront the person using them.

Group analysis applies psychoanalytic principles within the group. This involves a blank screen therapist who interprets emerging themes in terms of unconscious processes, including an exploration of group transference. It was one of the earliest group therapies, and established the basic expectations. These include the size of the group, with members sitting in a circle so that they can easily see each other, the duration of therapy (usually between one and two years), and the concept of what is called a *slow-open group*. Only rarely in analytic groups do members all start and finish at the same time—most join ongoing groups. As well as being practical, this has several real advantages for patients, such as being able to observe how other members deal with the end of their therapy before doing it yourself. Turnover needs to be modest so that group members can gain trust in each other and have the opportunity to pursue issues for a decent length of time.

Overall, however, the only predictable feature of group therapy is that it involves a group of people. Other than a belief that more can be learned by sharing and in the importance of confidentiality and boundaries, there is no single theory or set of rules or practices.

Groups can range from an analytical group for well-heeled intellectuals through to structured CBT groups for psychopaths in high-security prisons. Having said that, most group therapy encompasses a common set of processes.

Group processes

Irvin Yalom, a leading exponent of group psychotherapy, identified three underlying assumptions in group therapy. First, the central importance of *interpersonal relationships* for a robust sense of self. Second, that we can develop less distorted and more gratifying relationships through *corrective emotional experiences*. And finally, that the *social microcosm* of a group provides an ideal setting for *relearning*. As in life around us, group members will sooner or later recreate the same interpersonal universe they have always inhabited. A patient, abandoned by her mother and adopted into a high-achieving family with two children, had always felt of less value, that she was never going to fit in or be good enough. Finding it hard to trust relationships, she attacked them, creating the very rejection she feared. On joining a group she was antagonistic, instigated rows, and was often on the verge of leaving the group. Only this time round she was able to observe and change old patterns by using feedback from the other group members.

Group therapy offers an opportunity to get a better alignment between how we see ourselves and how we actually come across and are experienced by those around us. As Robert Burns put it, 'Wad some power the giftie gie us, to see ourselves as others see us.' A corrective emotional experience requires a new experience which is emotionally vivid, and where the emotions are clearly expressed. In a safe and supportive group feelings like anger or dislike can be expressed and feedback given honestly and openly. The ceiling doesn't fall in after all, the anticipated catastrophe does not materialize, and relationships are not destroyed. The second, and crucial, aspect of the experience is its cognitive processing, when group members can reflect on it. It is not enough just to feel something strongly, we need to make sense of the experience and see how it could change our future relationships.

Yalom also outlined several specific therapeutic factors in groups. These vary for different group members and over time, but tend to reinforce each other. *Group cohesiveness* is the foundation on which the group work rests. It corresponds to the therapeutic relationship in individual therapy, but includes the relationships of group members to one another, with the therapist, and also to the group as a whole. It is what makes the group attractive and keeps members attending, especially during the unfamiliar early phase. It makes the group feel comfortable and welcoming, similar to Carl Rogers' unconditional regard. Therapists and members have to work to sustain it. For the young adopted woman it made all the difference that she was warmly welcomed, was helped to say something about herself early on, and was not interrupted. Most importantly other group members found what she said helpful and told her so.

Upon this solid platform rests a range of therapeutic factors. *Installation of hope* arises from seeing that others with similar problems seem to be overcoming them. *Universality* is the sense that 'we're all in the same boat'. It reduces loneliness and shame, giving a sense of belonging to those who might otherwise withdraw from social contact. *Imparting of information*, such as the physical consequences of their habits in an eating disorder group, can make a surprising difference. A lack of basic knowledge and uncertainty are much more common than we often assume, and they make us anxious and less able to cope. The act of giving advice or information also demonstrates that others have our well-being at heart.

In groups, therapeutic activity does not originate from the therapist alone, but occurs naturally between group members. The sense of *altruism* this generates can be particularly therapeutic, as group members find they have something to offer others rather

13. We all bring our emotional baggage to therapy. In groups we are increasingly forced to leave this outside the room in order to deal with relationships in the here-and-now

than constantly feeling like they are a burden. Collectively, these processes enable members to share events and feelings they have rarely, if ever, told anyone about. Making such revelations can constitute another therapeutic factor, the *cathartic* experience.

Group members invariably bring old family conflicts and historical preoccupations into the group (see Figure 13), but the power of the group lies in the melting pot of the *here-and-now*. This is where the real interpersonal learning takes place. It is here that members become aware, through feedback and self-observation, of what they do to others and how, in turn, this rebounds on them. It is also where people can learn to see that they have the power, and ultimately the responsibility, to do something about it.

It's not all hard work. The group is a place to experiment with new ways of being and relating to others. These can be discovered by simply imitating others or by becoming aware of new feelings and ideas in the group. Groups provide an unparalleled opportunity to discover new and surprising aspects of yourself and your abilities. Simply accepting an offer of a tissue when talking about something upsetting can be liberating, just as finding yourself doing the same for another group member can be cathartic.

The group therapist will always return the attention of the group to the here-and-now, to the purpose of the group, and to the reason why each member is there. In addition to attending to what is being said, he will notice *how* things are expressed as well as enquiring into the *why*. With his experience the therapist also listens out for what is not being said or is being avoided, such as competitiveness or envy.

Interactive therapies

The therapies we will outline here occupy a special place in health services. They are all registered therapies, but in practice they often straddle the boundary between psychotherapy and a therapeutic activity. They may lack the specific characteristics of psychotherapy, such as an explicit agreement between a therapist and patient on the specific problems of an individual, and a relatively formal and tailored plan based on a detailed assessment. Obviously this is not a hard-and-fast divide—many psychotherapies are fairly open-ended in their initial goals, and individuals often discuss in detail what they want to gain from drama or music therapy, especially if provided in specialist settings or in private practice. In our experience however, it is rare for these therapies to be offered or sought independently of other treatment programmes within general mental health services.

Psychodrama

Psychodrama was initially created by Jacob Moreno in the early 1900s. He was equally frustrated with the overly formal, analytical approach of psychoanalysis, and with the strictures of the drama and theatre of his day. He stressed the need for spontaneity and improvisation to explore internal conflicts and painful memories, and to resolve unfinished business. Although it is group-based, psychodrama is essentially an individual approach, with one protagonist taking centre stage in each session. The group members are allotted different roles—for example, someone's powerful father figure—or act out different responses, such as one person challenging and another being more submissive. It has been widely used to explore family conflicts.

A typical session involves a number of people, helped by a 'director', to enable the protagonist to enact emotionally important scenarios of his choosing. After a warm-up to focus and enter a creative frame of mind, scenes are acted out. The protagonist is centre stage, but he can also invite others to take up his role (*mirroring*) or act as a double to put into words feelings he may only be dimly aware of, or be avoiding. Role plays and role reversals expand self-knowledge and perspective. The wind-up involves a discussion in which all the participants offer observations from the perspective of their allotted roles.

Drama therapy is a term used rather loosely to cover the use of drama to promote emotional awareness and personal growth. There have been a number of successful initiatives in prisons, as it recommends itself to men who are not used to talking about their feelings. Plays usually touch on the issues that matter powerfully to us, and often in dramatic and violent forms. Both acting and watching allows prisoners to identify with, and express their feelings through the actions of characters in a play.

Music therapy

Music therapy emerged in both the UK and the US in the aftermath of World War II in treatment programmes for soldiers recovering from physical and emotional injuries. It can be supportive and resource-building, but in Europe it is primarily psychodynamic, with musical improvisation at its core.

In a typical music therapy session therapist and client play together, in both senses of the word. The therapist will encourage the client to express her feelings through jointly creating music. Interacting with the therapist in this process, the client will often reveal her patterns of relating, initially with no need for words. No previous musical experience is needed. Instruments are generally provided, such as piano, guitar, drums, or xylophone, which are easy to use and highly expressive. The therapist is active and interactive, inviting an inhibited individual to exaggerate and let go of their feelings, or with others to contain and vary the expression of theirs. This can then be further explored through role play and discussion. The aim is to gain a fuller and less intellectual experience of the self, and to improve social interaction.

Music, perhaps more than any other art form, has the capacity to affect our emotions and mood. Even as infants we respond to the elements of music (timbre, pitch, volume, rhythm), and these still affect us as adults. Music's capacity to link with our more primitive or freer responses is used to full effect in music therapy. It is commonly used to help with communication difficulties in autism and learning disabilities, in reminiscence and orientation work with adults with dementia, with those recovering from strokes, and also in child and adolescent settings.

Art therapy

Art therapy has its roots both in art and in psychotherapy. It is used in two quite different ways, each prioritizing one of these origins. The first relies on the healing power inherent in the creative act of simply making art. The second uses the patient's art as the basis for interpretation in a more traditional psychotherapeutic format. What is created artistically is explored to enhance self-awareness and insight. Art therapy originally drew directly on psychoanalysis, but it became a profession in its own right in the mid-20th century. It can be used with individuals or groups.

In an art therapy session the aim is not to produce beautiful art, but rather to use a range of materials to create an image or a picture that speaks for an experience or a feeling state. As with music therapy it removes the reliance on words, but initially may have to overcome inhibitions: 'I'm no good at art' or 'I can't draw'. After the creative part of a session, time is usually spent discussing the personal meaning of what has been created or the materials used. Over time, or through a sequence of images, new meanings can be discovered or alternative feelings and identities experimented with.

All the interactive therapies we have described in this chapter make use of direct interpersonal experiences. This makes it possible to bypass some of the defences we described earlier, or at least for them to be identified and worked with at an early stage and with real immediacy.

We started this book with formal psychoanalysis, and have moved through time-limited therapies, CBT and counselling, to interactive therapies. We hope we have provided an overview of psychotherapy in its many different forms and current models. In the final chapter we will consider where psychotherapy goes next, and the challenges it faces in that process.

Chapter 8
Psychotherapy now and in the future

The 20th century has been called 'the century of psychiatry', and in many ways one could read that as 'the century of psychotherapy'. A hundred years ago, at the onset of World War I, psychotherapy had touched the lives of only a tiny number of people, and most of the population had simply never heard of it. Since then it has reached into almost every aspect of our lives—how we treat the mentally ill, how we understand our relationships, our appreciation of art and artists, and even how we manage our schools, prisons, and workplaces. Our culture has become one quite obsessed with understanding how people feel and our daily language is peppered with psychotherapy language.

What does the future hold? Have we witnessed the flowering of a cultural movement that is tied to just one unique time and place, or is it a fundamental step forward in human thinking and relationships? In our increasingly global world will it spread ever more widely or perhaps fade away altogether? Have the various changes in its practice made it more relevant to modern man or less so? Will the enormous advances in medicine, neuroscience, and psychology, and our move into the digital age of social media, render it obsolete?

How we judge psychotherapy's future will probably reflect what we think of it now: as a profound breakthrough in understanding ourselves and a step forward in social evolution, or as simply one among many technical procedures to reduce distress and improve human well-being. Reducing distress is certainly not a trivial achievement, but it does not satisfy psychotherapy's strongest advocates—they believe it has irrevocably changed the way we see the world and how we behave. From a different perspective, psychotherapy has been criticized right from the beginning for having 'cult-like' and religious overtones.

Psychotherapy or psychotherapies?

We have roughly divided psychotherapy's century into two halves. Up to the 1960s it was either psychoanalysis or one of its modifications. Therapies were verbal, protracted, and intensive, drawing on a detailed theory of unconscious forces. *Understanding* was the key to recovery. Later therapies have been much more experiential. Understanding remains important, but the *process* of psychotherapy and the *therapeutic relationship* have come to the fore. Some people are struck by the similarities between these psychotherapies and some by their differences. Are they adaptations of the same basic model or new and original approaches? It is a bit like deciding whether a glass is half full or half empty. Therapists usually stress the differences and the unique therapeutic mechanisms in their approach. Psychoanalysts and CBT therapists have traditionally had very little positive to say about each other's practice.

You may have found yourself drawn to one or other specific therapy. Alternatively you may come to the conclusion that they have more elements in common than divide them. The latter perspective is probably how we view things. Yes, CBT is undoubtedly radically different in tone, duration, and immediate focus from psychoanalysis. But both work by helping troubled individuals understand better the mental mechanisms that have caused and sustain their problems.

One thing the psychotherapies share is that they have all expanded their reach. The threshold for seeking psychotherapy or counselling has steadily lowered over the decades, and our demand for it seems inexhaustible. Their goals have also expanded—from just the reduction or removal of symptoms, towards self-fulfilment and well-being.

We can be certain that psychotherapy will undergo changes in both theory and practice. What is impossible to foresee is precisely where these changes will occur. The trend towards shorter, more structured and democratic therapies seems inexorable, but radical changes may come out of the blue. Will they come from developments such as computer science, or perhaps from other cultures than the Judeo-Christian origins of most current therapies? Prediction is a risky business.

Psychotherapy in medicine and psychiatry

It is easy to forget that psychotherapy originated within medicine, and that most of the early pioneers were doctors. They used psychotherapy to treat psychological disorders, but that did not mean that they ignored physical factors. The importance of biological considerations has waxed and waned but they never disappeared, and the medical hold on psychotherapy dominated until the 1970s. Some psychotherapies, especially in the Americas, were even restricted to medical practitioners, and departments of psychiatry were dominated by psychoanalysis. Since then psychologists and other non-medical practitioners have increasingly become the main force in providing counselling and psychotherapy. They now also lead most of the research and development.

Psychoanalysis paid a high price for its early dominance and undeniable hubris in the US, where it is now almost totally excluded from mainstream medicine. It has been replaced by an equally inflated and exaggerated reliance on pharmacological treatments. Outside the psychiatric mainstream however, psychotherapy remains widely available and very vigorous. In Europe, it always played a much smaller part in public psychiatry, and its rise and fall has therefore been nowhere near as dramatic. In the UK it is not the availability and influence of psychotherapy that has changed, so much as the type of psychotherapy and who delivers it. Now it is often provided by psychologists and is almost exclusively CBT. In parts of the UK CBT may be the only psychotherapy available in the National Health Service. A much wider range of psychotherapies is readily available in private practice and in other European countries.

Psychotherapy research

One of the reasons for psychotherapy's fading influence within medicine has been the increasing importance given to research findings. Medicine now sees itself as an evidence-based practice, rigorously assessing and comparing the effects of different treatments. Randomized controlled trials (RCTs) are considered the strongest test of a treatment. In an RCT patients are randomly allocated to either treatment A or treatment B (often a placebo, or dummy treatment), with neither the clinician nor the patient knowing which. The outcome is usually measured by an independent researcher. You can see how this provides very strong evidence, but also why it is incredibly hard to do in psychotherapy. It is almost impossible for patients, therapists, or researchers to be 'blind' to the treatment. Treatment also depends on sustained motivation by both therapist and patient. It is not like simply swallowing a pill, and there is bound to be variation in how individual therapists work.

Despite this many RCTs have been conducted in psychotherapy, although until more recently psychoanalysts have been unenthusiastic and generally uncooperative. The length of psychoanalysis clearly makes such trials particularly difficult, but the resistance also reflects many analysts' doubts about the research approach itself. After analysis a patient may be 'sadder but wiser'—is this better or worse? Such concerns are not unique to psychoanalysis. Much medical research has to make do with what can be measured, but the rewards of such pragmatism in terms of improved treatments are very obvious.

There are published trials in most of the psychotherapies, although the volume in CBT is dramatically greater. This does not mean that there is no research evidence that psychodynamic therapies also work, far from it. As research findings change rapidly, we will restrict ourselves to describing some well-established findings here. Today's cutting-edge results may be tomorrow's discounted news.

Overall the research confirms that most psychotherapies improve outcomes for patients compared to similar patients without therapy (usually those still on the therapy waiting list). Some studies have pitted one type of therapy against another but these are a minority. A surprising but consistent finding is that there is not that much specificity about the therapy (IPT is about as good as CBT, which is about as good as CAT, and so on). The evidence supports the importance of the quality of the therapy relationship and therefore of the so-called 'general factors' we have already discussed: genuineness, empathy, and non-possessive warmth. It is not quite that simple, however.

How, and by whom, therapy is conducted also seems to matter. More experienced therapists achieve better results, which is perhaps not surprising. However, therapists who stick closely to their model (whichever it is) also do measurably better. These two findings can seem contradictory. We might assume that more senior therapists get better results by being more flexible, but this is clearly not the full answer. Sticking to the model, to the agreed procedures if you will, and attending to the state of the therapy relationship, is what helps most.

While the body of research in psychotherapy is positive overall and generally points to *equivalence*, with skilled and thorough therapists getting broadly similar improvements, there are exceptions. Not only has more research been conducted with CBT, but it has demonstrated a clear superiority over dynamic therapies for some disorders. Often this is when the CBT therapists have adapted and refined their approach in a clearly targeted manner for individual conditions. These include depression, anxiety and panic disorders, and eating disorders.

So overall it is wrong to say, as many of its critics do, that there is no evidence that psychotherapy works. There is evidence. However, there is nowhere near enough. More good quality research is sorely needed if psychotherapy is to command continuing confidence and ensure public investment.

Psychotherapy in culture

While psychotherapy (especially psychoanalysis) has been in and out of favour in health care, it has kept going strong in our broader culture. Indeed, it is so strong that people often complain about excessive 'psychobabble' in public discourse. This is now being challenged by the rise of 'biobabble', which attempts to explain just about every possible human quality or behaviour with either evolutionary psychology or the neurosciences: 'we are hard-wired to…', 'your brain tells you to…', etc. Freudian language has been toned down, and some dated ideas on sexuality have long been abandoned. Stripped of their exaggerated language, analytic and psychotherapeutic ideas continue to permeate both high culture (such as the visual arts, novels, and the theatre) and popular culture (such as television, film, and the press). The language of emotional trauma, conflict, and defences frames our stories, with endless speculation about flawed relationships and human tragedies.

Globalism and multiculturalism

Psychotherapy and counselling are widely available for Westernized elites everywhere in the world. In the developing world it is less clear if these approaches are really accepted or relevant, even in adapted forms. Counsellors and psychotherapists are routinely confronted with the question of the cultural relevance and application of psychotherapy in our multicultural societies. Virtually every European country has around 10–15 per cent of its population born abroad, many with both a different mother tongue and a different set of values. In multicultural capital cities such as London or Copenhagen migrants can constitute half the population. There are some uncomfortable truths about access to psychotherapy. Wherever accurate figures on ethnicity are kept, ethnic minority populations are always over-represented as psychiatric patients but strikingly under-represented in counselling and psychotherapy services. They have more illness but get less psychotherapy. Can that be fair?

Much soul-searching goes into trying to understand this phenomenon. It was once thought that the higher rates of psychiatric diagnosis were due to misdiagnosis, but we now know this is not so. Being a migrant, especially a disadvantaged one, is highly stressful and causes more breakdowns. Those subject to such stresses should have a greater, not a lesser, need for psychotherapy, so why are they not getting it?

Two possible explanations exist with no clear answer. The first is that health-care staff fail to identify emotional and psychological problems in individuals with a different cultural heritage. They simply don't spot the cues. One example is that depressed patients with Pakistani and Indian backgrounds usually complain of tiredness and aches and pains, but only very rarely of sadness. Most counselling and psychotherapy services strive to be accessible to people from different cultures. They publicize their services in local places of worship and social centres, produce leaflets and posters in a range of languages, and provide interpreter services. This can reduce the barriers to access, but it does little to address the second possible explanation of the low uptake—that psychotherapy may not appear relevant or acceptable.

Whole books exist on how to provide culturally sensitive and effective counselling and psychotherapy. They debate whether to adapt practice, or keep faithful to the model but simply try harder. All agree that counsellors should find out about their clients' heritage and ask questions when unsure. White therapists should also be alive to the impact of their own ethnicity and to the power differentials in the relationship. Psychotherapy evolved in a privileged, white European and American environment, so they are at risk of taking its cultural assumptions too much for granted. Most black and Asian therapists have been sensitized to these concerns, which are now important components in most psychotherapy trainings.

A recurring question is whether to match the ethnicity of counsellor and client. If there is a common language this makes obvious sense, but otherwise opinions are divided. A therapist from the same background is likely to have a surer grasp of particular pressures and concerns, but she may have blind spots for just that reason. What if the problem lies in managing relationships with the mainstream culture? Or might a unique, personal concern get obscured by a focus on cultural issues?

Several psychotherapy services are run by counsellors from ethnic minorities specifically for their own communities. These fill an important gap but have not increased the overall take-up. There is also an uncomfortable concern that some form of service 'apartheid' could develop. As with women-only services, there is also a risk that problems will become externalized, creating a 'them and us' mentality shared by client and counsellor. This forges an immediate and strong bond, but could impede the examination of overall personal relationships in all their complexity and contradiction. Discussing these issues requires treading carefully to avoid opinions being tainted (or being thought to be tainted) with racism. There is no shortage of cultural imperialism in the history of psychiatry.

Psychotherapy in non-Western societies

We gave a very broad definition of psychotherapy at the start of this book: the deliberate use of a special, agreed relationship established between a trained practitioner and a patient to obtain relief from emotional suffering. This definition goes way beyond the practices we have traced from Freud in 19th century Vienna. Doing these different approaches full justice is not feasible in this short book. We shall restrict ourselves to some observations on how Western psychotherapy has adapted to other cultures, and been influenced by them.

These influences are not new. Eastern mysticism influenced Carl Jung at the very beginning of psychoanalysis. Currently, mindfulness-based cognitive therapy draws heavily on Buddhist thinking and practice. This focus on being *aware* of, and *accepting* the present moment and freeing yourself from past experience and future ambitions has been a persistent influence from Eastern philosophy. It is in striking contrast to the Freudian obsession with *understanding* and *changing*. At the time Freud was working in Vienna, Zen Buddhist exercises were used in Japan specifically to demonstrate how neurotic problems were absurd and inconsequential. In a worldview that discourages individualism, the patient was helped to 'let nature take its course'. Fritz Perl's gestalt therapy in the 1940s and 1950s embodied much of the same approach, although derived from European existentialism.

Think how different the Eastern emphasis on living vividly in the moment is to Freud's deferring of gratification. Some non-Western patients, less wedded to extreme individualism, often also want a more directive approach. They are happier to be instructed what to do, rather than be endlessly encouraged to decide for themselves. This difference is not just a reflection of a more hierarchical society. In much of the world people consider themselves first and foremost as a member of a family or a group, rather than as an individual. We Westerners are the odd ones out, and probably only for the last three or four centuries. Our psychotherapy embodies this view. For us, relationships are something we choose to engage in. They are important, but the starting point is always the individual. For most of the world the group we belong to (family or clan) is the starting point, more important than any individual ambition or career. The Zulu word *ubuntu* perhaps best conveys this. Widely used throughout Africa, the commonest translation is 'being a person through other people' or 'I am because we are'. It emphasizes the non-negotiable interdependence of all humans. We cannot be meaningfully understood as isolated individuals.

This fundamental difference in what it means to be a person has posed a massive challenge to counselling and psychotherapy, to which it is only now slowly responding. Will psychotherapy continue to evolve and adapt to this wider, more communitarian worldview? Or might globalization undermine the collectivism that has characterized much of the world up until now? Will it generate the same problems of extreme individualism, alienation, conflict, and isolation that we are so familiar with in the West, and with it a need for 'Western' psychotherapy?

Neurosciences and psychotherapy

Freud believed that advances in medicine would eventually do away with the need for psychotherapy completely. He certainly got that wrong. Psychotherapy and counselling have continued to flourish despite medicine advancing by leaps and bounds. Cutting-edge medical and cognitive neuroscience research is now confirming many of the underlying processes of psychotherapy and its benefits.

Some of the biological mechanisms that mediate relationships generally, and psychotherapy in particular, are now being identified. One striking example is the hormone oxytocin, the so-called 'bonding hormone'. Oxytocin is released both during breastfeeding and at orgasm. As well as promoting the flow of milk it has a direct and measurable effect on the mother's mood, generating a sense of contentment. If you give women or men oxytocin (it is absorbed easily in a nasal spray) they almost immediately report feeling contented. Even more striking, it makes them feel more positive towards whoever they are with at that moment—like the spell cast on the sleeping Bottom in Shakespeare's *A Midsummer Night's Dream*! The nursing mother is biologically confirmed in her attachment to her baby, and sexual partners have their relationship strengthened and deepened by a chemical swirling round in their blood. So our observations that the contentment and holding in psychotherapy allow us to experience those around us more positively may partly work through biological processes. This will come as no surprise to body psychotherapists.

Modern neuroscience has brought overwhelming confirmation of the unconscious mind. Experiments with computer images that last for microseconds show that our thinking, feeling, and behaviour are profoundly affected without us being in the least aware of what did it. These are not just trivial or nerdy effects. A subliminal computer image, or even word, can measurably change our view of whether someone is trustworthy or threatening. There is a certain poetic justice that this evidence for Freud's theory comes from ultra-scientific psychologists, most of whom would be deeply sceptical of everything he stood for. Neuroscience demonstrates just how widespread and essential unconscious processes are for healthy functioning. We simply could not get by without them. The Nobel Prize-winning psychologist Daniel Kahneman's book *Thinking, Fast and Slow* repeatedly confirms that we make the vast majority of our decisions using unconscious (often called intuitive) thinking. It is the rule rather than the exception.

Brain imaging has even begun to confirm physical effects of psychotherapy. Modern scanning techniques are extremely precise, so that differences in brain tissue size of less than a cubic millimetre can be measured. There are now a number of of studies measuring parts of the brain before and after psychotherapy. One of the earliest, in 1992, showed that treating depressed patients with either Prozac or CBT led to an equal increase in the volume of the caudate nucleus. Various parts of the brain (the amygdala, the hippocampus, and the frontal lobes) have been studied, as have various psychotherapies. Positive changes in one or other of these structures have been reported for most therapies. There is great excitement in this area of research, and we can expect many more findings. Some will undoubtedly be red herrings, but overall they do seem to confirm that there really is an interaction between the mind and the brain. This interaction goes both ways, and psychotherapy can influence it.

Conclusions

We hope this book has given you a sense of the richness and variety of psychotherapy. Human beings have always wanted to find meaning in their lives and to understand themselves and each other. The last century has seen a systematic attempt to understand our problems and to find specific ways of helping both those with severe disturbances and those with more common life-problems.

Psychotherapy and counselling occupy an uncomfortable place in modern medicine. They benefit from the enormous power of the scientific method to clarify their processes and to find 'what works for whom'. Yet this scientific approach feels at odds with their spirit. Science measures what we have in common and ignores what makes each of us different. We have to be treated as 'cases' to advance scientific knowledge, but none of us wants to be treated as 'a case' in our own therapy. What matters to us is the unique, personal experience of transformation that comes from two individuals working together. These two are not simply interchangeable with any other two other individuals.

Luckily researchers are becoming more skilled at making the necessary adaptations to test psychotherapy processes without losing this essence. Such research has confounded the sceptics and confirmed that psychotherapy does work. It does help people to change and get better, it is not just a matter of time healing. This research has also consistently shown that the quality of the therapy relationship is of essential importance, and how crucial training and skills are.

We now have a range of therapies from which to seek help. They are no longer an exclusive and expensive prerogative of the ultra-rich and the intellectual. Most therapists are registered with professional bodies, which provides reassurance about their training and skills, although you need to check. As the stigma about psychological problems and their treatment has receded, people now talk openly about their therapy, and can recommend who and what helped and what did not. Psychotherapy may be challenging, but it needn't be feared and its results can be life changing. We believe it will be here for the foreseeable future.

References

The triangles discussed in Chapter 2 were inspired by David H. Malan, *Individual Psychotherapy and the Science of Psychodynamics* (Butterworths, 1979).

In Chapter 3 we mention John Bowlby's book *Maternal Care and Mental Health* (Jason Aronson, 1977).

The Nina Coltart quotation in Chapter 3 is from *The Baby and the Bathwater* (Karnac Books, 1996).

The Jung quotation in Chapter 3 is from his memoirs, *Memories, Dreams, Reflections* (Pantheon Books, 1963).

The Angela Molnos quotations in Chapter 4 are from *A Question of Time* (Karnac Books, 1995).

The Anthony Ryle quotation in Chapter 4 is from Anthony Ryle and Ian B. Kerr, *Introducing Cognitive Analytic Therapy: Principles and Practice* (Wiley, 2002).

The books by Carl Rogers mentioned in Chapter 5 are *On Becoming a Person* (Houghton Mifflin, 1961) and *A Way of Being* (Mariner Books, 1980).

In Chapter 7 we refer to Robin Skynner's *One Flesh, Separate Persons: Principles of Family and Marital Psychotherapy* (Constable, 1976).

The Salvador Minuchin quotation in Chapter 7 is from *Families and Family Therapy* (Tavistock Publications Limited, 1974).

Daniel Kahneman's book, mentioned in Chapter 8, is *Thinking, Fast and Slow* (Allen Lane, 2011).

Further reading

This book is only a brief overview of the main types of psychotherapy and counselling. There are literally countless books on the subject at all levels of complexity. Here we present a very limited list of books that we have either found stimulating and informative, or which give an accessible background to the issues raised.

Pat Barker, *Regeneration*, Penguin, 1991.
The first novel in her *Regeneration Trilogy*, describing the emotional trauma and psychotherapeutic treatment of shell-shocked soldiers in WW1. The central figures are the poets Siegfried Sassoon and Wilfred Owen, as well as fictional characters.

Eric Berne, *Games People Play: The Psychology of Human Relationships*, Penguin, 1964.
A short, engaging, and best-selling introduction to transactional analysis by its originator. Still fresh, and with vivid descriptions of many of the patterns we get stuck in.

Tom Burns, *Psychiatry: A Very Short Introduction*, Oxford University Press, 2006.
An overview of psychiatry which helps place the development of psychotherapy in its professional context.

Gillian Butler and Tony Hope, *Manage Your Mind: The Mental Fitness Guide*, Oxford University Press, 2007.

An easy and practical guide to self-help using the whole range of psychotherapy skills, with an emphasis on those used in CBT.

Gillian Butler and Freda McManus, *Psychology: A Very Short Introduction*, 2nd edition, Oxford University Press, 2014.
An authoritative introduction to psychology as a science and a profession.

Mick Cooper, *Essential Research Findings in Counselling and Psychotherapy: The Facts are Friendly*, Sage, 2008.
A comprehensive and accessible summary of research findings and their implications for psychotherapy practice.

Colin Feltham, *What's the Good of Counselling and Psychotherapy?* Sage, 2002.
A series of perspectives on all aspects of psychotherapy, from target problems and ethics through to its broader achievements.

Sue Gerhardt, *Why Love Matters, How Affection Shapes a Baby's Brain*, Brunner-Routledge, 2004.
An accessible, if detailed, interpretation of relevant recent findings in neuroscience and psychology. Probably for the more committed reader.

Stephen Grosz, *The Examined Life: How We Lose and Find Ourselves*, Chatto and Windus, 2013.
Tales drawn from the day-to-day practice of an experienced psychoanalyst, which capture the essence of the analytic experience and the stories people need to tell.

Jeremy Holmes, *John Bowlby and Attachment Theory*, Routledge, 1993.
An in-depth yet readable presentation of John Bowlby and his theories, brought to life through vivid clinical vignettes by this prolific commentator on psychotherapy.

Adam Phillips, *Winnicott*, Fontana Modern Masters, Fontana Press, 1988.
An introduction to the life and work of Donald Winnicott by a well-known psychotherapist and essayist. Readers would benefit from prior background understanding of analytic concepts.

Anthony Roth and Peter Fonagy, *What Works for Whom? A Critical Review of Psychotherapy Research*, Guildford Press, 1996.
A most comprehensive compilation of research evidence for psychotherapies. Very authoritative but mainly for professionals.

Robin Skynner and John Cleese, *Families and How to Survive Them*, Mandarin, 1984.
A best-selling self-help book co-authored by a psychotherapist and a comedian. It takes the form of dialogues between the two and is both educational and amusing.

Anthony Storr, *The Art of Psychotherapy*, 2nd edition, Butterworth Heinemann, 1990.
A humane and profound account of the process of psychotherapy, mainly aimed at those in training or in related fields.

Anthony Storr, *Freud: A Very Short Introduction*, Oxford University Press, 1989.
A comprehensive and readable account of the man and his developing theories. It offers a nuanced critique rather than simply a chronological outline.

Elizabeth Wilde McCormick, *Change for the Better: Self-Help Through Practical Psychotherapy*, Sage, 2012.
A self-help book using easy conversational language, arranged around the ideas of CAT. Relevant for anyone interested in how we become who we are and how to improve things for our troubled selves.

Mark Williams, John Teasdale, Zindel Segal, and Jon Kabat-Zinn, *The Mindful Way Through Depression*, Guilford Press, 2007.
A resource for learning about mindfulness drawing on meditative traditions and cognitive therapy, complete with a CD of guided meditations.

Irvin D. Yalom, *The Gift of Therapy: Reflections on Being a Therapist*, Piatkus, 2001.
An honest and engaging account of various aspects of the psychotherapeutic process, reflecting Yalom's respectful stance to his patients and his work.

Index

Expand your collection of
VERY SHORT INTRODUCTIONS

ONLINE CATALOGUE
A Very Short Introduction

Our online catalogue is designed to make it easy to find your ideal Very Short Introduction. View the entire collection by subject area, watch author videos, read sample chapters, and download reading guides.

http://fds.oup.com/www.oup.co.uk/general/vsi/index.html

SOCIAL MEDIA
Very Short Introduction

Join our community

www.oup.com/vsi

- Join us online at the official Very Short Introductions **Facebook** page.
- Access the thoughts and musings of our authors with our online **blog**.
- Sign up for our monthly **e-newsletter** to receive information on all new titles publishing that month.
- Browse the full range of Very Short Introductions online.
- Read **extracts** from the Introductions for free.
- Visit our library of **Reading Guides**. These guides, written by our expert authors will help you to question again, why you think what you think.
- If you are a teacher or lecturer you can order inspection copies quickly and simply via our website.